Evaluation and the Federal Decision Maker

Gerald L. Barkdoll, *Editor*
University of Southern California

James B. Bell, *Editor*
James Bell Associates

NEW DIRECTIONS FOR PROGRAM EVALUATION
A Publication of the American Evaluation Association
A joint organization of the Evaluation Research Society and the Evaluation Network

MARK W. LIPSEY, *Editor-in-Chief*
Claremont Graduate School

Number 41, Spring 1989

Paperback sourcebooks in
The Jossey-Bass Higher Education and
Social and Behavioral Science Series

Jossey-Bass Inc., Publishers
San Francisco • London

Gerald L. Barkdoll, James B. Bell (eds.).
Evaluation and the Federal Decision Maker.
New Directions for Program Evaluation, no. 41.
San Francisco: Jossey-Bass, 1989.

New Directions for Program Evaluation Series
A publication of the American Evaluation Association
Mark W. Lipsey, *Editor-in-Chief*

Copyright © 1989 by Jossey-Bass Inc., Publishers
and
Jossey-Bass Limited

Copyright under International, Pan American, and Universal Copyright Conventions. All rights reserved. No part of this issue may be reproduced in any form—except for brief quotation (not to exceed 500 words) in a review or professional work—without permission in writing from the publishers.

New Directions for Program Evaluation is published quarterly by Jossey-Bass Inc., Publishers (publication number USPS 449-050), and is sponsored by the American Evaluation Association. Second-class postage rates are paid at San Francisco, California, and at additional mailing offices. POSTMASTER: Send address changes to Jossey-Bass Inc., Publishers, 350 Sansome Street, San Francisco, California 94104.

Editorial correspondence should be sent to the Editor-in-Chief, Mark Lipsey, Psychology Department, Claremont Graduate School, Claremont, Calif. 91711.

Library of Congress Catalog Card Number LC 85-644749

International Standard Serial Number ISSN 0164-7989

International Standard Book Number ISBN 1-55542-874-6

Cover art by WILLI BAUM

Manufactured in the United States of America. Printed on acid-free paper.

Ordering Information

The paperback sourcebooks listed below are published quarterly and can be ordered either by subscription or single copy.

Subscriptions cost $60.00 per year for institutions, agencies, and libraries. Individuals can subscribe at the special rate of $45.00 per year *if payment is by personal check*. (Note that the full rate of $60.00 applies if payment is by institutional check, even if the subscription is designated for an individual.) Standing orders are accepted.

Single copies are available at $14.95 when payment accompanies order. (California, New Jersey, New York, and Washington, D.C., residents please include appropriate sales tax.) For billed orders, cost per copy is $14.95 plus postage and handling.

Substantial discounts are offered to organizations and individuals wishing to purchase bulk quantities of Jossey-Bass sourcebooks. Please inquire.

Please note that these prices are for the calendar year 1989 and are subject to change without prior notice. Also, some titles may be out of print and therefore not available for sale.

To ensure correct and prompt delivery, all orders must give either the *name of an individual* or an *official purchase order number*. Please submit your order as follows:

Subscriptions: specify series and year subscription is to begin.
Single Copies: specify sourcebook code (such as, PE1) and first two words of title.

Mail orders for United States and Possessions, Latin America, Canada, Japan, Australia, and New Zealand to:
Jossey-Bass Inc., Publishers
350 Sansome Street
San Francisco, California 94104

Mail orders for all other parts of the world to:
Jossey-Bass Limited
28 Banner Street
London EC1Y 8QE

New Directions for Program Evaluation Series
Mark W. Lipsey, *Editor-in-Chief*

PE1 *Exploring Purposes and Dimensions,* Scarvia B. Anderson, Claire D. Coles
PE2 *Evaluating Federally Sponsored Programs,* Charlotte C. Rentz, R. Robert Rentz
PE3 *Monitoring Ongoing Programs,* Donald L. Grant

PE4	*Secondary Analysis,* Robert F. Boruch
PE5	*Utilization of Evaluative Information,* Larry A. Braskamp, Robert D. Brown
PE6	*Measuring the Hard-to-Measure,* Edward H. Loveland
PE7	*Values, Ethics, and Standards in Evaluation,* Robert Perloff, Evelyn Perloff
PE8	*Training Program Evaluators,* Lee Sechrest
PE9	*Assessing and Interpreting Outcomes,* Samuel Ball
PE10	*Evaluation of Complex Systems,* Ronald J. Wooldridge
PE11	*Measuring Effectiveness,* Dan Baugher
PE12	*Federal Efforts to Develop New Evaluation Methods,* Nick L. Smith
PE13	*Field Assessments of Innovative Evaluation Methods,* Nick L. Smith
PE14	*Making Evaluation Research Useful to Congress,* Leonard Saxe, Daniel Koretz
PE15	*Standards for Evaluation Practice,* Peter H. Rossi
PE16	*Applications of Time Series Analysis to Evaluation,* Garlie A. Forehand
PE17	*Stakeholder-Based Evaluation,* Anthony S. Bryk
PE18	*Management and Organization of Program Evaluation,* Robert G. St. Pierre
PE19	*Philosophy of Evaluation,* Ernest R. House
PE20	*Developing Effective Internal Evaluation,* Arnold J. Love
PE21	*Making Effective Use of Mailed Questionnaires,* Daniel C. Lockhart
PE22	*Secondary Analysis of Available Data Bases,* David J. Bowering
PE23	*Evaluating the New Information Technologies,* Jerome Johnston
PE24	*Issues in Data Synthesis,* William H. Yeaton, Paul M. Wortman
PE25	*Culture and Evaluation,* Michael Quinn Patton
PE26	*Economic Evaluations of Public Programs,* James S. Catterall
PE27	*Utilizing Prior Research in Evaluation Planning,* David S. Cordray
PE28	*Randomization and Field Experimentation,* Robert F. Boruch, Werner Wothke
PE29	*Teaching of Evaluation Across the Disciplines,* Barbara Gross Davis
PE30	*Naturalistic Evaluation,* David D. Williams
PE31	*Advances in Quasi-Experimental Design and Analysis,* William M. K. Trochim
PE32	*Measuring Efficiency: An Assessment of Data Envelopment Analysis,* Richard H. Silkman
PE33	*Using Program Theory in Evaluation,* Leonard Bickman
PE34	*Evaluation Practice in Review,* David S. Cordray, Howard S. Bloom, Richard J. Light
PE35	*Multiple Methods in Program Evaluation,* Melvin M. Mark, R. Lance Shotland
PE36	*The Client Perspective on Evaluation,* Jeri Nowakowski
PE37	*Lessons from Selected Program and Policy Areas,* Howard S. Bloom, David S. Cordray, Richard J. Light
PE38	*Timely, Lost-Cost Evaluation in the Public Sector,* Christopher G. Wye, Harry P. Hatry
PE39	*Evaluation Utilization,* John A. McLaughlin, Larry J. Weber, Robert W. Covert, Robert B. Ingle
PE40	*Evaluating Program Environments,* Kendon J. Conrad, Cynthia Roberts-Gray

New Directions for Program Evaluation

A Quarterly Publication of the American Evaluation Association
(A Joint Organization of the Evaluation Research Society
and the Evaluation Network)

Editor-in-Chief:

Mark W. Lipsey, Psychology, Claremont Graduate School

Editorial Advisory Board:

Scarvia B. Anderson, Psychology, Georgia Institute of Technology
Gerald L. Barkdoll, U.S. Food and Drug Administration, Washington, D.C.
Robert F. Boruch, Psychology, Northwestern University
Timothy C. Brock, Psychology, Ohio State University
Donald T. Campbell, Social Relations, Lehigh University
Eleanor Chelimsky, U.S. General Accounting Office, Washington, D.C.
James A. Ciarlo, Mental Health Systems Evaluation, University of Denver
Ross F. Conner, Social Ecology, University of California, Irvine
William W. Cooley, Learning Research and Development Center, University of Pittsburgh
David S. Cordray, U.S. General Accounting Office, Washington, D.C.
Robert W. Covert, Evaluation Research Center, University of Virginia
Lois-Ellin Datta, U.S. General Accounting Office, Washington, D.C.
Barbara Gross Davis, Educational Development, University of California, Berkeley
Howard E. Freeman, Sociology, University of California, Los Angeles
Egon G. Guba, Education, Indiana University
Edward S. Halpern, AT&T Bell Laboratories, Naperville, Illinois
Harry P. Hatry, The Urban Institute, Washington, D.C.
Michael Hendricks, MH Associates, Washington, D.C.
Gary T. Henry, Joint Legislative Audit and Review Commission, Virginia
Dennis H. Holmes, Education, George Washington University
Ernest R. House, CIRCE, University of Illinois, Urbana-Champaign
Jeanette M. Jerrell, Cognos Associates, Los Altos, California
Karen E. Kirkhart, Social Work, Syracuse University
Henry M. Levin, Education, Stanford University
Richard J. Light, Government, Harvard University
Charles McClintock, Human Service Studies, Cornell University
William A. McConnell, San Francisco Community Mental Health Programs
Jeri Nowakowski, Leadership and Education Policy Studies, Northern Illinois University

Michael Q. Patton, International Programs, University of Minnesota
Charles S. Reichardt, Psychology, University of Denver
Leonard Rutman, Price Waterhouse Associates, Ottawa, Ontario
Thomas A. Schwandt, Center for Educational Development, University of Illinois, Chicago
Penny Sebring, NORC, University of Chicago
Lee Sechrest, Psychology, University of Arizona
Jana Kay Slater, California State Department of Education
Midge F. Smith, Agricultural and Extension Education, University of Maryland
Nick L. Smith, Education, Syracuse University
Robert E. Stake, CIRCE, University of Illinois, Urbana-Champaign
Robert M. Stonehill, U.S. Department of Education
Daniel L. Stufflebeam, Evaluation Center, Western Michigan University
Robert St. Pierre, Abt Associates, Inc., Cambridge, Massachusetts
Carol H. Weiss, Education, Harvard University
Joseph S. Wholey, School of Public Administration, University of Southern California
Paul M. Wortman, ISR, University of Michigan
William H. Yeaton, ISR, University of Michigan

American Evaluation Association, 9555 Persimmon Tree Road, Potomac, MD 20854

Contents

Editors' Notes 1
Gerald L. Barkdoll, James B. Bell

1. **Evaluation and the Political Appointee** 7
Ronald H. Carlson

Experienced political appointees candidly describe the barriers to effective management that they want evaluators to help them overcome.

2. **Program Managers: Victims or Victors in the Evaluation Process?** 15
Richard C. Sonnichsen

Career government executives report how they feel (and how they would like to feel) when they hear "Hi, I'm an evaluator, and I'm here to help you."

3. **Evaluation and Congress** 27
Michael E. Fishman

Members of congressional staffs identify six "windows of opportunity" for evaluators who want to influence legislative decision making.

4. **Increasing Client Involvement in Evaluation: A Team Approach** 35
Christopher G. Wye

An experienced evaluator explains how to use a team approach to solve the problems of tight timeframes and the need to develop a data base from scratch.

5. **Three Techniques for Helping International Program Managers Use Evaluation Findings** 49
Robert Werge, Richard A. Haag

International programs are used as a setting to describe techniques that will also prove effective in domestic evaluations.

6. **Advice for the Evaluated** 57
Joseph N. Coffee

An experienced organizational development specialist presents frank advice for program managers who want to (or have to) work with evaluators.

7. **Process Dimensions in Program Evaluation** 71
Ray C. Oman

This chapter offers a summary of the social, political, and interpersonal dimensions of evaluation.

Index 79

Editors' Notes

Life was simpler for early evaluators. They developed (or borrowed) analytical methodologies and tools, which they applied to public programs as they encountered them. Of course, early evaluators did not recognize that the life they were living was simpler, because they had no reference points for comparison. In addition, their work did not seem at all simple at the time, because they were actively discussing and debating sample size, internal validity, confounding variables, and other technical issues. Their life became much more complicated, however, when one of them asked a disturbing question: "If part of our job is to measure the effectiveness of programs and activities, isn't it appropriate that we also measure the effectiveness of our own activities?" The answer was obviously yes; but when the effectiveness of current evaluation efforts was measured, the results were discouraging. The most notable outcome of these early self-assessments were exquisitely detailed taxonomies of reasons why evaluations had no impact.

During subsequent discussions of impact, utilization, and effectiveness, evaluators discovered a common denominator in many of the failures: the client. Over time, it became obvious that there were many factors related to the client (and the evaluator's relationship with the client) that helped determine whether the evaluator's work was put to use. Since then, evaluators have been actively exploring the client side of evaluation. To date, we have learned that understanding and managing the interpersonal, organizational, and political dimensions of the evaluation process are at least as important and difficult as understanding the analytical dimensions of evaluation methodology.

This sourcebook is intended to add to the growing body of knowledge about clients, who come from myriad organizational settings with a wide array of expectations, biases, values, problems, and previous experiences with evaluation. It presents information about three types of decision makers who are frequently clients of evaluation: career government executives (frequently referred to as program managers), political appointees, and members of congressional staffs. The insights presented into the different characteristics of these decision makers demonstrate the subtle but often significant differences among these three types. Though our focus is on federal decision makers, our experience suggests that we also provide some clues about the characteristics of evaluation clients at the state and local levels.

The significant challenge for evaluators is to determine whether they can use what they are learning about clients to foster more effective use of evaluation in public decision making. We urge other researchers to add to this important body of knowledge.

This Sourcebook's Development

This volume reflects the unique activities that produced it. For the past three years, a group of senior evaluators and others interested in the field have met monthly to discuss evaluation activities, processes, techniques, successes, and failures. This forum was established by Joseph S. Wholey at the Washington Public Affairs Center of the University of Southern California. These meetings typically involved ten to twenty people, lasted two hours, and included presentations by two members of the group, followed by discussion and debate. The first year's discussions (1985-86) became the basis of a book (Wholey, 1987) and a panel discussion at the 1986 ASPA national conference. Similarly, the 1986-87 meetings produced a second book (Wholey, Newcomer, and Associates, 1989) and a second ASPA panel.

In the absence of Wholey's leadership, while he was on sabbatical in 1987-88, a small planning group decided to add another dimension to that year's meetings. In effect, the group said, "For the past two years, we have spent a great deal of time talking about our perceptions of our clients' wants and needs. Let's ask them to give that information to us directly. Let's try to see ourselves and our activities as our clients see us."

The first three meetings of that season were devoted to collecting the views of the three types of decision makers, one meeting for each type. A total of eleven decision makers attended these meetings. Decision makers who attended represented a variety of functions and responsibilities. A complete list is included at the end of this introduction.

The decision makers all agreed that they had been clients of evaluators, and every one of them had a great deal to say. They candidly shared their expectations, experiences, concerns, and criticisms. Some of what they said was unpleasant for the evaluators to hear, but all of it was informative and valuable. The clients were glad for the opportunity to talk about their experiences, and some even described the sessions as cathartic.

The evaluators who attended those first three meetings were later moved to a great deal of activity and reflection. Some of them took on the job of documenting, organizing, and analyzing the clients' comments. Others set about developing or refining their ideas about how to make evaluation activity more relevant to clients' needs, expectations, and criticisms. A third group identified and documented case studies of successful evaluation activities related to the clients' comments. These efforts produced a rich agenda for subsequent meetings and lively sessions at the

1988 ASPA national conference and the 1988 AEA national convention. They also inspired contributions to this sourcebook.

The Sourcebook's Organization

The first three chapters describe the three types of decision makers. Ronald H. Carlson (Chapter One) focuses on political appointees, Richard C. Sonnichsen (Chapter Two) examines career government executives (program managers), and Michael E. Fishman (Chapter Three) looks at committee staffs as key agents in congressional decision making. These chapters cover decision makers' working environment, clients' relationship with staff offices and how it affects their relationship with evaluators, and types of information that clients need for effective decisions. All three authors augment the information directly provided by participating decision makers with relevant information from secondary sources, comments made by participants at ASPA conferences, and information collected through phone conversations and informal discussions with others knowledgeable about these types of evaluation clients. In short, the materials presented in the first three chapters provide an opportunity for readers to understand what decision makers have in common and how they differ.

The second half of the volume continues the exploration of evaluators' clients from several perspectives, including:
- Examples of evaluators meeting clients' needs through creative and innovative approaches
- Special challenges for evaluators who work with clients in international settings
- Advice that consultants can give to clients who are working with evaluators
- The process dimensions that an evaluator can modify or influence to ensure productive evaluation.

The following "previews of coming attractions" briefly describe each of the chapters in the second half of the volume, to help readers identify chapters of particular interest.

Christopher G. Wye (Chapter Four) offers a cogent description of an imaginative approach to a very difficult assignment. The program being evaluated was politically sensitive and of direct interest to high-level political appointees and career executives. It had to be evaluated within a short time and required the development of an original data base. Wye describes what happened and then draws inferences from the experience, which should help evaluators who find themselves in similar situations.

The international perspective, presented by Robert Werge and Richard A. Haag (Chapter Five), provides a powerful metaphor for evaluators to use in considering the organizational and interpersonal dimensions of an evaluation. The authors suggest that an evaluation is in many ways like a visit to a foreign country. The power of this metaphor is doubled because it is relevant both to the evaluator and to the program manager experiencing the language, customs, behavior, and values of the other for the first time. The techniques the authors describe for overcoming the challenges of evaluation in international settings will also be of considerable interest to evaluators working in domestic environments that feel like foreign countries.

Joseph N. Coffee's contribution (Chapter Six) is as thought-provoking as some of the concerns and criticisms we heard from career executives, political appointees, and staff members. An experienced organizational development consultant, Coffee is very pragmatic about the good and bad characteristics of evaluators. He asserts that evaluators come with all levels of technical competence, with a wide variety of ethical standards, and with differing levels of interpersonal skill. Coffee's chapter will be very helpful to evaluators who want to see themselves as others see them. His advice to program managers is orderly, detailed, and specific, and evaluators looking for insights and suggestions will appreciate his perspective.

Ray C. Oman (Chapter Seven) gives a convenient summary of the many process variables that an evaluator must consider in designing and conducting an evaluation. Oman has organized them into a logical taxonomy that evaluators can use to ensure that they have covered all the bases.

We are barely beginning to delve into ways of distinguishing types of clients and responding to these differences so that evaluations can contribute more. Several hours of discussion among a relatively small group of evaluators and clients cannot be expected to yield definitive conclusions. Nevertheless, we hope we have focused attention on some meaningful issues and that forthright and earnest discussion among senior evaluators and decision makers will have led to better evaluations.

> Gerald L. Barkdoll
> James B. Bell
> Editors

References

Wholey, J. S. *Organizational Excellence: Stimulating Quality and Communicating Value.* Lexington, Mass.: Lexington Books, 1987.

Wholey, J. S., Newcomer, K. E., and Associates. *Improving Government Performance: Evaluation Strategies for Strengthening Public Agencies and Programs.* San Francisco: Jossey-Bass, 1989.

Gerald L. Barkdoll is associate commissioner of the U.S. Food and Drug Administration and is adjunct professor at the University of Southern California. Dr. Barkdoll received the Myrdal Award for Government Service and the Presidential rank of Meritorious Senior Executive. His research and practice focus on the organizational, cultural, and political knowledge and skills needed by successful evaluators.

James B. Bell is director of James Bell Associates, a firm specializing in applied program evaluation. Formerly he was a member of the Urban Institute's Program Evaluation Studies Group. His current efforts focus on Medicaid and Medicare, rural health care, military dependent and retiree health coverage, and biomedical research resources.

To meet the needs of politically appointed program managers, evaluators need to overcome organizational and evaluation-related barriers.

Evaluation and the Political Appointee

Ronald H. Carlson

The Changing Political Environment and Evaluation

Periodically, the federal government witnesses the arrival of a new group of politically appointed executives, who report to work under the auspices of a new administration. The new leaders experience culture shock and a bureaucratic trauma as they are suddenly faced with a complex environment of systems, legislative and regulatory requirements, and a different way of doing things. It is a phenomenon in government as predictable as the changing of the palace guard; in most respects, that is what it is. The difference, of course, is that it is not just a new group of people but also a new set of policies cloaked in the political mandates to be implemented during the administration's time in office. The mission for these politically appointed executives is to "deliver the goods," and to do it within the rules and regulations of the federal bureaucracy.

This chapter is about the evaluation aspect of this managerial and program challenge as new political leaders develop and seek to carry out their work. Evaluation is one of the key elements of this challenge. Those who are carrying out the mandate for accomplishing the political agenda must know whether the key goals and objectives integral to the mandate are being developed and implemented effectively.

Setting the Scene: Evaluation and the New Client

The meeting with the political appointees at the Washington Public Affairs Center made clear the importance that those clients place on the value of good, timely information. In response to a question about what would make their lives as managers more productive, one of them said, "If a genie were to appear in my office, and if I were trying to manage a program more effectively, I would want the genie to provide me with a system that tells me everything I need to know about the delivery of our programs. I have a lot of information, but not what I feel I must have, especially regarding whether those programs are doing what they are supposed to do in helping people." Only with that type of feedback, this person went on to say, can a manager know how to implement, reshape, or restructure a program to accomplish the mandate, obey the law, and even exceed goals and objectives.

The objective of a manager, these clients said, is to find and use information to ensure good program development and effective management. Evaluators can help in meeting that objective if they understand what is needed, and if managers understand how evaluation can be used productively. As another client pointed out, "Evaluators need to help trigger new and creative thinking."

The clients described what they believe is a strong market for better information. The demand, they said, far exceeds the supply in nearly every aspect of political appointees' tenure. Talking about this "information and evaluation deficit," the political appointees identified two categories of barriers that contribute to the deficit: those that are administrative and organizational, and those that are specific to evaluation management and resource availability.

Administrative and Organizational Barriers

The political appointees commented broadly on the number of barriers that limit the effective management of public programs whose managers are also trying to accomplish a political mandate. They cited a number of general obstacles that affect the evaluation aspect of their jobs.

Lack of Discretionary Authority. As the government's legislative branch and its committee structure have become larger and more complex, few programmatic areas have not become subject to legislative and regulatory directives. The intensity of such legislative activity has resulted in what these managers characterized as Congress's "micromanagement" of most programs. Such activity ranges from the defining of types of data to be collected to the very production of reports. This micromanagement, they believe, leaves new executives with few opportunities to introduce policy changes, even at the level of program operations. A "mandate for leadership," with new political agenda requiring quick action, is held back by managers' lack of discretionary authority.

Unwanted Influence of Congressional Committees. Another problem is the weight and influence of the congressional committees and especially of the congressional committee staffs. Unlike political appointees in the administrative arm of government, congressional staffers do not confront certain organizational, programmatic, and legislative barriers. When Congress wants information, it can order evaluations and special reports, either by calling for them in appropriations or authorization legislation or by going directly to one of its service organizations, such as the General Accounting Office, the Congressional Budget Office, or the Office of Technology Assessment. When such legislatively mandated activities are conducted under the direction of the opposing political party, there can be even greater barriers for political appointees who may also be seeking information—often on similar questions, but from another perspective. This counterquestioning, given the barriers confronting the executive, provides the legislative branch with a head start on the evaluation of important policy issues.

Administrative and Contracting Impediments. To ensure equity, fairness, and competitiveness in the government's procurement of consultants' services, rigorous rules and regulations have been set down by the General Services Administration and the several departments within the administrative branch of the government. The executives who were interviewed saw this environment as a "millstone" around the manager's neck. Professional consultation is frequently needed from outside organizations, given its general unavailability from parts of the line organizations. Unfortunately, to get access to outside help, the manager must adhere to the process set out in the government's contracting requirements. There are often many long delays before a qualified organization can begin work on an issue.

Lack of Familiarity with Programs and Organizational Structure. The culture shock felt by most political appointees usually coincides with the introduction of myriad symbols, acronyms, and other bureaucratic shorthand, but the new language is only incidental to the arrival of volumes of program data in which new executives find themselves immersed. As one of the interviewed managers observed with some annoyance, "I frequently find myself drowning in data and starved for information." Moreover, organizational directories may be as thick as the Manhattan telephone book. The manager discovers, often with unbridled impatience, the difficulty of accomplishing any significant task in a timely way.

Lack of Good, Timely, and Reliable Information. Federal programs frequently include reporting systems for outside organizations (for example, state and local government and private-sector grantees). Information is often unavailable for several months after an event, because of delays in data collection and presentation. Therefore, managers' ability to answer questions quickly is greatly limited. The Office of Management and Budget, for example, imposes specific guidelines for the collection of information from more than ten outside organizations. These guidelines are intended to ensure that any request for data is strictly necessary, but they can produce delays of many months, depending on the complexity and the policy significance of the information to be collected.

Evaluation-Related Barriers

The clients also identified evaluation-related obstacles that they believe stand in the way of getting useful returns on investment in evaluation.

Weak Evaluation Skills. The political appointees talked at length about the need for strong evaluation skills. They admitted that many new managers come to their assignments inadequately equipped with management skills and experience, but they also found a general lack of strong evaluation skills throughout the career service. When one of the clients was reminded that outside contracting is always available to provide technical skills, he quickly pointed out, "Unless you have a competent internal group to work with, you won't understand good evaluation when you see it." In his opinion, a set of basic skills must be present in every organization, and one of these skills is the ability to design and produce useful evaluations.

Unaccountability of Some Staff Members. A recurring criticism was that too many program analysts in the career service lack any significant program and performance accountability. The political appointees speculated that professional bureaucrats do not believe being accountable to political leaders is necessary, because of frequent turnover and disruptive transitions. Program analysts are sometimes perceived as having little or no incentive to become trusted advisers to new managers and help them carry out the mandates set by political leaders. Two clients commented that to cope with this problem the new manager must establish a good rapport with staff members and take advantage of differing points of view. They emphasized the importance of understanding staff members and their backgrounds, since some of them might well have been involved in creating the very programs now viewed as unnecessary, too costly, or ineffective. Another political appointee took this issue to the extreme of saying that some conflicts could be eliminated if staffs were simply reduced: "Too many staffers produce nothing of value. The agencies could get rid of 90 percent of their professional evaluation staffs and be much better off."

Conflicting Evaluations. In the opinion of the political appointees, too many program- and policy-based evaluations are at odds with the political agenda. If caution is not used, evaluation issues may be raised and studies may be undertaken that present conflicts, contradictions, and even embarrassments to the new mandate. For example, an evaluation of a program that the new administration has declared unnecessary, unwanted, and not requiring public support could be a political bombshell if the evaluation produced information appearing to justify some level of continuing public support. Without caution, such an evaluation produces information at odds with the philosophy espoused by the political appointee. Such a phenomenon is perhaps unavoidable, given the cycling and recycling of policy- and program-based questions, which often overlap administrations. For example, some of the major reforms sought by the Reagan administration called for the elimination of many domestic programs that had been funded at least over the previous decade. The new administration clearly intended to shift the Washington policymaking machine into conservative gear. While that was happening, however, studies that had been undertaken earlier were being completed, and sometimes they produced conflicting information that made the new job more difficult.

Unwillingness of Career Managers to Work in the Political Process. The political appointees observed that many professionals operate to control information and influence policy, in a way that is inherently in conflict with the efforts of politically appointed managers. Career evaluators and analysts are trained to solve problems by applying science and rationality. Politicians, in contrast, approach problems through negotiation and compromise. Thus, political appointees often may seem to be untrained people who do not know how to solve problems rationally. The dynamics of this phenomenon can produce conflict over the best way to influence the production of the information that will eventually be used to bring about change. As one of the interviewed clients pointed out, "You have to keep your roles and relationships with evaluators clear and well understood. Your job is to ask evaluators what is meaningful, but then you have to use the information so that it meets the stated needs for the new budget and program-development goals."

Improving Things

The political appointees all recognized the importance of relevant information and the potential contribution that evaluators can make. They also recognized substantial barriers. They named three actions that they believed would have contributed effective management of their own programs and offered them as advice to future political appointees.

1. Rapidly build a trusting and mutually supportive relationship

between new political appointees and incumbent evaluators. If this proves impossible with incumbents, make prompt staff changes.
2. Persuade key political and career managers that information is crucial to decision making. One political appointee said, "Identify the major decision points in the organization, especially points where decisions have political consequences, and assign a competent evaluator to provide useful information systematically on key issues."
3. Show evaluators that to contribute accurate, timely information to political appointees will not require them to play politics or assume bias.

One political appointee summarized her peers' feelings when she said, "We, as program managers who are here because of our respective political appointments, have to be responsible and do the very best job we can. To do that means making a strong and continuing resource commitment to all aspects of program evaluation."

A Final Observation

The colloquy with the political appointees underscored three principles that should guide evaluators who work in a politically driven world. Certainly the foremost of these principles, emphasized repeatedly, is to establish supportive relationships with political appointees in a way that demonstrates understanding of their particular program goals and objectives. The second principle is to accept that in a political environment, while basic program missions will remain the same, goals and objectives will probably ebb and flow, depending on the political process. The third principle is to maintain a balanced set of relationships, so that evaluators are not seen as either endorsing or advocating a political agenda, and at the same time to support appointees in their mandates. Many evaluators may feel as if they are trying to work in the maddening world of *Alice in Wonderland*. It may not be the world of Lewis Carroll's Alice, but it is the kind of work environment where an evaluator, to be effective, needs to be politically astute, flexible, and technically competent (not necessarily in that order).

Participants

Career Government Representatives

John Kelso
Deputy administrator, Health Resources and Services Administration
Department of Health and Human Services

Rhoda Davis
Associate commissioner, Office of Supplemental Security Income,
Social Security Administration
Department of Health and Human Services

Mike Suzuki
Associate commissioner, Office of Program Development,
Administration on Aging/Department of Health and Human Services

Frank Ferro
Former deputy associate commissioner, Children's Bureau
Administration for Children, Youth, and Families

David E. Bucher
Director of Trademark Examining Operations,
Patent and Trademark Office
Department of Commerce

Political Appointees

James E. Colvard
Deputy director, Office of Personnel Management
Former deputy chief, Navy Materiel Command

Glenna Crooks
Pagonis and Donnelly Group, Inc.
Former deputy assistant secretary for health,
Department of Health and Human Services

Arlene Triplett
McManis Association
Former assistant secretary for administration, Department of Commerce

Congressional Representatives

Douglas Campbell
Fleishman Hillard
Former counsel, Committee on Labor and Human Resources

Doug Cook
Group Leader, National Security, U.S. Senate Budget Committee

Norm Chlosta
Deputy chief, Resource Management and Evaluation,
Office of Pesticide Programs, Environmental Protection Agency
Former policy analyst, Senate Budget Committee

Ronald H. Carlson is associate administrator for the Office of Planning, Evaluation, and Legislation in the Health Resources and Services Administration. His research activities while in the Department of Health and Human Services were in health services and financing demonstration and evaluation projects.

Federal program managers want evaluation information, but they also want evaluators to develop greater empathy and understanding.

Program Managers: Victims or Victors in the Evaluation Process?

Richard C. Sonnichsen

Evaluation, unfortunately, is often viewed metaphorically as a sporting event, with victims and victors among the players. The outcome, like beauty, lies in the eye of the beholder, with divergent perspectives represented by evaluators and program managers. The purpose of this chapter is to describe the perspective (including resentment and frustration) of senior-level career government executives toward evaluations and evaluators. It is hoped that illuminating this perspective and the relationships it engenders will contribute to improvements in the practice of evaluation.

The data and observations in this chapter are based on the views of a panel of executive-level federal program managers assembled at the Washington Public Affairs Center (WPAC), University of Southern California (USC); the experiences of the evaluation staff of the Federal Bureau of Investigation; and a 1976 symposium jointly sponsored by the National Institute of Law Enforcement and Criminal Justice and the MITRE Corporation.

The Evaluators' Perceptions

The evaluators who meet monthly at WPAC are experienced and successful in their field. Over the past two years, they have discussed and debated the organizational, methodological, and cultural dimensions of evaluation. By most standards, they would be considered enlightened and informed with respect to the views of senior-level program managers, their clients for many years. Their perceptions are described here as a backdrop to the presentation of what they later heard from visiting executives.

The evaluators' views of evaluation activities can be presented from three perspectives: as they view evaluation and their role in it, as they view program managers and their perceptions of evaluations, and as they view the inherent stress and conflict of the evaluation process.

Evaluators' Views of Evaluation. The purpose of evaluating government programs is relatively straightforward: to serve the needs of decision makers in both the legislative and executive branches of government and furnish them with information on performance for policy formulation, policy execution, and accountability (Chelimsky, 1985). It is the execution of this purpose that causes conflict, jeopardizes the use of evaluation, and engenders animosity toward evaluators among program managers.

Two conditions exist in most evaluation settings (Sonnichsen, 1989). First, no program is perfect or functioning optimally, and an evaluator will always develop suggestions to improve it. Second, an externally suggested improvement is interpreted as an implicit deficiency in the program and is resisted by program personnel.

If there were no managers, programs, or activities, there would be little need or demand for evaluation. At the risk of overstating the obvious, it is incumbent on evaluators, in the practice of their profession, to garner understanding and empathy for the program managers who constitute the raison d'être of evaluation and are primary clients of evaluators' work.

The ability to communicate, influence, and persuade is not a quantitative skill but a behavioral adaptation used by evaluators during their encounters with program managers, clients, and stakeholders in the evaluation setting. The initial encounter between the evaluator and the program manager, after the announcement of an evaluation, is a structured contact. Although it produces uncertainty, it takes place within certain understood rules and traditions of the organization. The reactions of program managers to announcements that their programs will be evaluated depend significantly on the historical sphere of influence of the evaluators.

The design and conduct of a successful evaluation, often thought of as a methodological issue, depends on the interpersonal and communication skills of individual evaluators. The interaction of the evaluation staff with other organizational entities during evaluation is a complex social arrangement that depends on numerous internal and external factors but is significantly affected by the relationship between the evaluator and the line manager responsible for the program being evaluated.

Evaluators' Views of Program Managers. Laboring in the government vineyard as a manager, responsible for implementing and operating legislatively based programs, is a difficult task. Translating sometimes vague but ambitious legislation into workable programs that meet the intentions of diverse stakeholders borders on the impossible; yet, every day, thousands of dedicated public administrators commit their energies and skills to this endeavor.

The scrutiny of the activities of governmental program managers can be intense. In the interest of accountability and efficiency, they are subjected to review by all three branches of the government and by public-interest groups. Managers must satisfy the interests of Congress, act within the strictures of the courts, perform efficiently and effectively for their own superiors, and provide redress for the problems of citizens. Given the diverse stakeholders' interests that intrude on the operations of program managers, it is no wonder that the announcement of an evaluation causes anxiety.

Many evaluators view program managers as obstacles to their research efforts and see them as unappreciative of elegant methodology, opposed to change, and lacking interest in either program review or recommendations for improvement.

Evaluators' Views of Stress and Conflict. Washington, D.C., is the scene of a peculiar ritual that takes place regularly in federal agencies. An evaluator from an office of evaluation greets a manager in charge of a program: "Hi, I'm an evaluator, and I'm here to help you. I'm going to evaluate your program." Responding diplomatically, the program manager, with dissembled enthusiasm, says, "We're glad you're here, and we'll cooperate in any way we can." Thus concluded, this quaint and disingenuous ritual signals the beginning of another program evaluation. A formality, this initial encounter between evaluator and manager does little to disguise the hostility and conflict that can be generated during an evaluation.

Over the past two decades, evaluation has become a widespread management methodology for determining the intent, efficiency, and performance of federally funded programs. Paradoxical in application, it is a management technique designed to improve performance while at the same time critically judging it. This inherent conflict in the practice of evaluation tends to polarize viewpoints on this management technique in the minds of evaluators and program managers, with each side occupying opposite ends of the evaluation spectrum. Seen by most evaluators as a powerful management technique to bring fresh insight and new perspectives to problems and redirect attention from routine daily rituals to important program issues, evaluation is typically viewed by program managers as an unbeneficial intrusion into their sphere of responsibility. Program managers, however, are not uninterested in sound management practices, nor do they disagree with the concept of improved performance as the goal of evaluation. Their concern is often based on the intrusive process of evaluation—the way evaluation is conducted and the use of its results.

While evaluation should be viewed as a reflexive encounter between the evaluator and the program manager, program managers see it as a device designed to detect inefficiencies in their operations. Evaluators see it as a rational, scientific approach to enlightened management, but program managers see it as threatening and introducing uncertainty into a stable process. With competing goals and differing views of the evaluation process, evaluators and program managers create conflicts that permeate all aspects of an evaluation.

The essence of program managers' concern is the uncertainty generated by their limited influence before and during the evaluation process and by their lack of clear understanding of the use of findings and results. This lack of control, coupled with a perceived lack of evaluators' accountability and their perceived detachment from programs, forms the basis of program managers' aversion to evaluation.

The uncertainty of evaluators' approach tends to put program managers on the defensive. Some evaluators view themselves as critics; others are genuinely interested in helping program managers overcome obstacles and improve their operations. Determining, at the outset of an evaluation, the type of evaluator he or she is dealing with is of primary interest to the program manager.

The program managers' perspective was eloquently and forcefully presented by four distinguished career government managers in September 1987 to the seminar at WPAC. The comments of the program managers fall into four categories, related to staff versus line functions, accountability, evaluation offices' placement, and data-collection methodology and use.

Staff Versus Line Functions

These program managers saw evaluation as imposed on them, by forces external to their programs, and used in a judgmental fashion to gauge the performance of their programs. The following comments by panel members clearly express the emotion generated by an evaluation, as well as the general disenchantment with staff offices: "If I couldn't do away with staff offices, I would certainly minimize their day-to-day interference, and that would include evaluators, too." "We create in our bureaucracy a system of staff-to-line operations that by definition creates tension." "If you look at organizations, you find that there are at least as many staff people as there are program people, and in many cases there are far more staff people than program people, and it doesn't make sense." "The thing that gets me is the work load that staff offices generate for line operations. As the line manager, I cannot see any relevance to the mission we have."

Clearly audible in these remarks is the lack of differentiation between evaluation and other staff functions: The program managers' antipathy toward administrative organizational functions is equally directed to evaluators. This failure to separate evaluation from other administrative burdens helps to explain the resistance that evaluators encounter from program personnel.

Accountability

Program managers are very sensitive to their role as providers for services or products, for which they are held accountable. They are judged by quality and volume of output and must maintain and efficiently use their resources. Any demand for these resources that does not directly contribute to a program's mission is viewed as a burden. Evaluators, who are not seen as accountable for agencies' productivity, are relegated to the "burden" category, as evidenced by the following comments: "Evaluation offices think they're program offices and want to run the program. You don't want to evaluate it, you want to tell programs what to do and yet not be held accountable." "They absorb resources but don't produce anything. They are not responsible. Ultimately, no staff officer is ever held accountable for what a program office does. Evaluators are competitors for program direction and resources."

Thus, the purposes and uses of evaluation are deemed oppressive and intrusive, no matter how benevolent the actions of evaluators. This perception, together with the resource demand during evaluation and the occasional use of program money to fund evaluation, engenders animosity between evaluators and program managers.

Evaluation Offices' Placement

In the eyes of program managers, evaluation is threatening. Managers view evaluators as having greater access to agency executives: In many federal organizations, evaluators are placed above program managers in the hierarchy and report to assistant secretaries. Evaluators' loyalties are seen as directed up the organizational hierarchy, and they are seen as having little empathy for program personnel and their missions. The technique of evaluation is onerous to program managers, but the organizational placement of evaluation offices and the purposes of evaluation also precipitate consternation, as evidenced by these comments: "The researchers were too far away from the program to understand the distinctions, much less the results of the program." "When evaluators evaluate, they seem to march to a different drummer, so you really feel frustrated." "It's almost like I'm on earth and you're on Mars." "An improvement would be more control and closer proximity of the evaluation office to the program."

Although the placement of the evaluation office—away from the program manager, and not under his or her control—contributes to the gap between evaluators and program personnel, a close inspection of the managers' comments reflects a communication gap more than a concern with the physical placement of evaluation offices. Distance and communication problems cause misunderstandings that drive a wedge between evaluators and managers and inhibit successful evaluations.

Data-Collection Methodology and Use

Panel members at the WPAC seminar also wanted increased input into the data-collection effort and a voice in its eventual use for judging performance. A line manager is required to furnish program data to evaluators, which may then be used to demonstrate to agency executives and congressional funding bodies that the program is not functioning optimally.

Program managers believe that superficial analysis of numbers to describe programs is often used by political appointees to advance administration policy, whether or not the program is having the desired effect. Contributing to this phenomenon is the difficulty of measuring the impact of governmental social programs. Lacking impact data, Congress and the incumbent administration tend to fixate on easily obtainable numbers. Once begun, the publishing of this data is difficult to undo, particularly if an annual incremental increase in the program numbers can be used to demonstrate that an administration policy is working. This approach to program review obscures actual impact and leads to resentment among program managers, as evidenced by the following comments: "We need good data, but we should be very involved in the definition of what those data needs are, and they should not be imposed on us." "You feel you are not always measured against what you think are the relevant objectives of your program."

A common lament heard from program managers was that easily obtained data tend to obscure the real impact and performance of programs. They observed that fixation on numbers by agency executives and congressional committees precludes deeper examination of programs. According to them, the numbers generated by evaluation tend to measure outputs rather than outcomes. They believe that overemphasis on numbers often has the unintended consequence of misdirecting programs.

The 1976 Symposium

The issues raised, and the intensity and emotion displayed by the program managers at the WPAC seminar, are no recent phenomena. A

1976 symposium on the use of evaluation by federal agencies produced similar observations. The symposium examined the success of program evaluation in federal agencies at producing information, as well as the extent of its use by the executive and legislative branches of government for developing and implementing policy. A positive conclusion was reached by the seminar participants, representing nine federal agencies: "Evaluation is not only the necessary foundation for most other efforts to assess the worth of services provided by the government, it is certainly the best currently available method for producing reliable information on the effects of social programs" (Chelimsky, 1977, p. 51). Notwithstanding this conclusion, however, the symposium cautioned that careful consideration was needed in organizing the evaluation function, to accommodate the viewpoints of program managers on the uses of evaluation findings. The placement of the evaluation function in organizational structures was also raised at the symposium, but no consensus was reached: The independence gained by centralization may be offset by resistance to evaluation findings, but accommodating program managers by placing the function at the program level may jeopardize the independence of evaluation. The symposium participants also determined that using evaluation to establish accountability runs the risk of bureaucratic inertia. They said that program managers have enough tools and opportunities at their disposal to prevent the implementation of recommendations, if these are considered threatening.

Four controversial areas identified at the symposium highlight the polarization between evaluators and program managers:

- The difficulty of using the social research model to address agency requirements for relevance, responsiveness, and timeliness in the evaluation product
- The failure of the current agency incentive structure to reward managers for the effectiveness of their programs or for their efforts to improve effectiveness via evaluation
- The arduousness of reconciling different evaluation perspectives, expectations, and information needs among different evaluation users, so that information produced for one user can satisfy the needs of another
- The awkwardness of selecting implementation mechanisms that simultaneously reduce threats to managers and increase knowledge.

Debate during the symposium produced a recommendation for increased communication among evaluators, program managers, and policymakers. Conferees felt that careful consideration of the viewpoints of program managers was necessary to increase the use of the evaluation product.

Despite the program managers' complaints about evaluation, their comments indicate more concern with the process than with the concept.

Although managers are zealous and parochial toward their programs and dedicated to accomplishing their goals, they showed no lack of interest in information about program operations, but they were concerned about the ultimate uses of the information. Useful facts, presented in a nonjudgmental fashion, that would help improve program performance would be welcome. Managers' fear of evaluation was grounded in evaluators' possibly incomplete understanding of program activities. Evaluators must heed this not-so-subtle message and try to accommodate the views and concerns of program managers when conducting evaluations. This challenge presents an opportunity for evaluators and program managers to develop areas of understanding that will foster productive evaluation practices to benefit both parties. If agreement exists on the concept of evaluation but conflict is common during evaluation, the participants must focus on the process itself.

Evaluation Practice

The issues raised by the WPAC panel participants and the symposium attendees are significant and must be addressed by evaluators and program managers alike if evaluation is to be used effectively and if evaluators hope to influence the activities, directions, and goals of programs. The failure of evaluation to be productive and useful often stems from evaluators' detachment from the mainstream of organizational life and from their unfamiliarity with the responsibilities and needs of program managers. The environment of the evaluator is also the organization's. To practice evaluation successfully in this environment implies a thorough knowledge and understanding of agencies' rubrics, cultures, decision-making processes, important actors, and political structures. Evaluators have long lamented the lack of acceptance of their work, many times reproaching program managers for their failure to recognize its value. Program managers in turn charge evaluators with lack of empathy and misunderstanding of their working environments. Resistance to evaluation among program managers has its genesis in the purposes of evaluation (as seen by program managers), the way evaluations are conducted, and the use or misuse of evaluation findings.

To be successful, evaluators must position themselves as links rather than barriers between program managers and top management. Evaluation should be viewed by those it serves and by those it reviews as an essential element of the administrative mechanism of an organization (Sonnichsen, 1988). Evaluation can operate as an interface between the operating activities of an organization and its upper-level management, furnishing information (in both directions) to be used to alter, adjust, and improve program activities. This is a "people" process: evaluators interacting with managers to determine operating efficiency and effectiveness. Evaluation, however, is a judgmental process, and success depends largely on mutual understanding between program managers and evaluators on the purposes and goals of each side's mission.

In attempting to increase the use of evaluation through better understanding between evaluators and managers, neither party should overlook evaluation's potential to be misused by political appointees interested in rapid implementation of their own agendas. This is a factor that can affect program managers and evaluators alike. For example, Sanera (1984) boldly states, "Policy evaluation is a key instrument, uniquely suited to the purposes of conservative government, but it is currently underutilized. Properly employed, policy evaluations can be used for two purposes: to bring about policy change within government programs, and to combat the growth of government by demonstrating the wasteful and destructive nature of expansion government" (p. 541). Awareness of such attempts to subvert legitimate management-review functions, such as evaluation, is the first step toward preventing this type of abuse. The practice of evaluation is significantly affected by the biases and attitudes of the participants, which in turn affect their behavior. Only by recognizing and understanding these phenomena can evaluators proceed with some hope of impact.

Conclusion

The use of evaluation to determine the efficacy of public programs is still mired in controversy. Program managers continue to resist evaluation efforts, and evaluators lament the lack of acceptance of their work. The issue remains: Does evaluation help or hinder the operations or activities of line managers? Are they victims of the evaluation process, or are they victors?

They are neither. A review of the program managers' comments reveals the belief that they have little to gain from evaluation. More significant, however, is the failure of the program managers to differentiate between evaluators and other staff members. It may be disquieting for evaluators to learn that what they view as a scientific, rational, sophisticated management approach to judging the performance of programs is viewed by program managers in the same light as budget, personnel, and other administrative burdens that separate line and staff operations. This lack of distinction between evaluation and other organizational and administrative functions offers insight into managers' resistance to evaluation.

A powerful and important message to evaluators can be distilled from these comments. Three major themes can be detected. First, program managers would welcome the information that evaluators can provide if it were gathered and presented in a less hostile format. Second, program managers fear the uncertainty surrounding the use of evaluation results. Third, the anxiety of program managers, brought on by traditionally aloof evaluation practices, can turn into behavior that defeats their own desire for program data.

The essence of their message is fairness. The program managers seem to be saying:

- Allow us more involvement in the evaluation process.
- Honestly convey the purpose and the uses of evaluation.
- Present a balanced perspective on programs by portraying successes as well as deficiencies.
- Remember that program managers are clients of evaluation.

This chapter has attempted to demonstrate the arguments used by program managers to resist evaluation, and it sets out their rationale for this position. Although the material in this chapter comes from the federal perspective, the problems encountered are not unique to the federal sector but are generic evaluation dilemmas also found in state and local environments.

Evaluation, because it is viewed in most environments as an intrusive and threatening management tool, has not reached optimum utilization, nor has it gained acceptance as an integral function of most public agencies. Criticism of the process, however, should not be construed as damning the concept of evaluation; it should be seen as an opportunity to review the process constructively and advance the concept of evaluation as an effective management tool and increase its use. The views of program managers presented in this chapter are emotional but not vituperative. The managers made eloquent and fervent entreaties, requesting evaluators to develop greater empathy and more understanding of the role of program managers in the delivery of public services.

Collaborative efforts are enhanced when there is genuine interest in a mutual goal—in this case, increased organizational effectiveness. Using evaluation to accomplish this task, however, creates a burden for evaluators. Their task is to market both themselves and their product. Progress in the practice and use of evaluation will require joint recognition by evaluators and program managers of the goals, aspirations, and impediments peculiar to each party's endeavor, as well as a convergence of their positions. It will be a reciprocal process of learning and listening. The payoff is a mutual goal: increased performance and ability of the government to deliver services to its citizens.

References

Chelimsky, E. *Analysis of a Symposium on the Use of Evaluation by Federal Agencies.* Vol. 2. McLean, Va.: MITRE Corporation, July 1977.

Chelimsky, E. "Old Patterns and New Directions in Program Evaluation." In E.

Chelimsky (ed.), *Program Evaluation: Patterns and Directions.* Washington, D.C.: American Society for Public Administration, 1985.

Sanera, M. "Implementing the Mandate." In S. M. Butler, M. Samera, and W. B. Weinrad (eds.), *Mandate for Leadership II: Continuing the Conservative Revolution.* Washington, D.C.: Heritage Foundation, 1984.

Sonnichsen, R. C. "Advocacy Evaluation: A Model for Internal Evaluation Offices." *Evaluation and Program Planning,* 1988, 2 (1).

Sonnichsen, R. C. "Using Evaluation to Stimulate Program Change." In J. S. Wholey and K. E. Newcomer (eds.), *Improving Government Performance: Evaluation Strategies for Strengthening Public Agencies and Programs.* San Francisco: Jossey-Bass, 1989.

Richard C. Sonnichsen is deputy assistant director of the Inspection Division, Federal Bureau of Investigation, Washington, D.C., where he heads the Office of Program Evaluations and Audits. He has a B.S. degree from the University of Idaho and is a doctoral candidate in public administration at the University of Southern California. His areas of interest are internal evaluation and evaluation utilization.

Despite constraints and obstacles, evaluators have opportunities and ways to increase the use of evaluation findings in legislative decisions.

Evaluation and Congress

Michael E. Fishman

How is evaluation used in congressional decision making? What in the legislative environment either uniquely promotes or discourages the use of evaluation? What issues should evaluators be sensitive to while working in this environment? My evaluation group sought answers to these questions from three senior congressional committee staff members, who were invited to share their views with our evaluation group. In addition, a literature review turned up several articles and books on Congress's use of evaluation and analysis.

This chapter briefly describes evaluation use in Congress, in the hope that evaluators will find the information helpful in understanding Congress as a client for evaluation. The chapter begins with a description of general characteristics of the congressional environment that seem to influence the nature of evaluation use. Next, it provides a brief summary of specific constraints on evaluation use, including those stemming from evaluators. Finally, opportunities for evaluation use are discussed, as well as implications for evaluators who want to take advantage of these opportunities.

Any views expressed in this chapter are those of the author and should not be construed to represent the official position or policy of the U.S. Department of Health and Human Services.

The Congressional Environment

The congressional committee staff directors described their environment as highly political, partisan, and fast-moving. There are 535 members of Congress, each of whom represents his or her own constituency and political party and seeks reelection every two or six years. Each piece of authorizing legislation and each bill appropriating money for the operation of the federal government requires a majority vote in both the House and the Senate. The members are extremely busy people, and the pace of legislative activity can be very fast.

As a result, congressmen and senators rely heavily on their staffs to help them process an enormous volume of information and to monitor the complex legislative process. These information-filtering functions are prominent enough for some observers to have suggested that congressional staff are an invisible and unelected legislature. As one scholar notes, however (Zweig, 1979), "most staff are careful not to take the boss's place or to inordinately assume that authority has been delegated to them. After all, congressional staff serve at the pleasure of their bosses."

Congressional staff work in at least three different venues. First, each member of Congress has personal staff members, who attend to constituents and legislative interests. The focus of these staff tends to be either handling constituents' requests for assistance or working on specific legislative issues of interest to the member, based on the special needs of his or her district or state and on his or her committee memberships. Second, each congressional committee and subcommittee (a total of about 275 groups) has its own staff. As staff directors for key committees, the individuals we interviewed play a critical role in the development of legislation, its progress through Congress, and the congressional oversight process. Therefore, they probably are typical of key clients for evaluation information in a legislative setting.

Given the important role played by congressional committees and their staffs, it is useful to understand that the committee structure is complex and overlapping. It is not unusual for more than one committee to be interested in a program or an issue. Each committee is staffed by persons selected by its chairperson, representing the majority, and by the ranking minority member of the committee. A committee or subcommittee chairperson's personal staff may sometimes play a key role in specific legislative issues, but committee or subcommittee staff members are often the most knowledgeable about their own specific areas of legislative responsibility.

Congress also has several bipartisan analytical-support organizations. While they are not the focus of this chapter, it is important to mention the roles played by the General Accounting Office (GAO), the Congressional Budget Office (CBO), the Congressional Research Service (CRS), and the Office of Technology Assessment (OTA). GAO conducts audits and evaluations of executive-branch programs and others. CBO provides nonpartisan analysis of the budget and other resource issues of interest to Congress. CRS provides both short- and long-term analytical services on a wide range of issues. OTA provides analysis and evaluation of long-term policy issues, particularly those likely to have significant technological or environmental consequences.

Constraints on the Use of Evaluation

The committee staff directors whom we interviewed reported notable constraints on more thoughtful use of evaluation in the legislative process: the overly partisan tone of congressional debate, the lack of cooperation and information sharing between the legislative and executive branches, and the lack of statesmanship among individual legislators facing reelection. Weiss (1987) defines similar barriers in terms of political ideology and organized interests, to which no issue is value-neutral. Furthermore, she lists structural issues that make the use of analysis by congressional committees difficult. These include specific committees' tendency to become advocates for the programs they authorize, as well as the tangled web of committee jurisdictions, the limited time and energy of members, and the hectic pace of legislative activity. She also acknowledges that committee members tend to want confirmation of their own judgments, which staffers are often anxious to reinforce, and that the style of operation is one of bargaining and compromise rather than rational calculation.

The committee staff directors also named constraints on evaluation use that stem from evaluators. They noted that much of the evaluation and analytical information they receive is poorly packaged and irrelevant to the intended audience or to the issue immediately at hand. Committee staff members also value clear analytical assumptions and caveats, because parties on each side of an issue carefully scrutinize the claims and arguments of others who take positions on the issue. Congressional staffers rely on the quality of their information, and because weak arguments can be quickly exploited, credibility can be harmed by inaccurate information. The credibility of information is often judged more by its source than by its substance, partly because of underlying concern that there are no professional standards for evaluation.

Opportunities for Evaluation

What opportunities exist for the use of evaluation information by congressional decision makers? The congressional staff directors identified six "windows of opportunity" for evaluators seeking influence over legislative decision making.

Development of New Legislation. Congressional authorizing committees and special committees often conduct hearings in search of legislative remedies. This process provides an opportunity to present evaluation results to committee staffs and even to testify on results before appropriate subcommittees. The development of new legislation is usually a slow process that provides ample time for an evaluator to identify issues and deliver information. For example, in January 1986, the president called for a study of the national welfare system. In addition to an administration study, several studies developed recommendations. The House and Senate each conducted hearings during 1987, passed welfare reform bills in 1988, and in September 1988 reached final compromises in conference, which resulted in enactment of the Family Support Act of 1988. Research and evaluation related to the dynamics of welfare participation and to the effects of education, training, and work programs on welfare recipients played a significant role in the development of this new legislation.

Reauthorization of Existing Legislation. Many domestic programs are authorized by legislation that has an expiration date. Continuation of a program beyond that date requires reauthorization or reenactment of legislation. Reauthorization is managed by the relevant authorizing committees in the House and Senate. This process gives evaluators notice of when information will be needed, and by whom. It has the added feature of an action-forcing deadline. There may be disagreement on what form reauthorization will take—how, if at all, the program should be changed—but there is usually agreement that the program should continue. This leads to a process that is often compressed around the expiration of an existing statute.

Annual Appropriations and Budget Cycle. Each year, Congress establishes an overall federal budget, with specific amounts earmarked for each area where federal funds are to be spent by the executive branch. Budget deficits and major differences in spending priorities between a Republican president and a Democratic Congress have intensified an already highly charged process. Nevertheless, both the budget and appropriations processes provide some opportunities to present evaluation information. In this context, however, the committee staffs involved will be less highly specialized than staffs of authorizing committees, and the process will provide less time for consideration of new ideas. The committee staffers we interviewed described the budget process as "broad brush" and the appropriations process as "fast-moving and highly partisan."

Oversight Hearings. Congressional committees often hold oversight hearings on existing federal programs. These hearings provide an opportunity to assess and evaluate both the performance and the federal management of these programs. Oversight hearings provide a unique opportunity for congressional review of programs that do not have a fixed statutory life. For entitlement programs, such as Social Security and Medicare, oversight hearings are held frequently and offer a predictable opportunity for the presentation of evaluation results.

Congressionally Mandated Evaluations. It is not uncommon for Congress to mandate, in authorizing legislation or in appropriations language, that the executive branch conduct a specific evaluation. This is a clear signal that information on a program or an issue is wanted. There is generally a one- to three-year turnaround time on such requests.

Expansion of the Body of Knowledge. Congressional committees have an ongoing need for new information related to their areas of interest. Evaluation results that are judged to add to this body of knowledge are likely to have an important influence on what becomes accepted standard knowledge. In the often fast-paced congressional environment, information accepted as common knowledge may prove more influential than late-breaking evaluation results.

The committee directors we interviewed made it very clear that, despite these "windows of opportunity," the actual congressional policy and decision process is often anything but predictably deliberative and rational. As Zweig (1979) notes, decisions are often reached through political bargaining and compromise rather than through reasoned review of facts and policy alternatives.

Implications for Evaluators

How can evaluators be effective in a legislative environment? Our congressional staff interviewees believe that evaluators must tailor their information to meet the specific needs of specific congressional staffers at specific times. For evaluation information to be useful in the legislative process, it must be:

- Timely—available to staffers when they need it
- Relevant—presented so that it directly addresses the issue under consideration and the legislative process that is occurring
- Professional—with all assumptions stated and all appropriate disclaimers included
- Well packaged—clearly and succinctly communicating the facts in terms relevant to the current debate and to the knowledge levels of the staffers involved.

The development of new legislation affords an opportunity to assemble and present complex information over an extended period. Detailed study results can be shared with congressional staffers who are working to fashion legislative responses to identified issues. The credibility of evaluators can be established in ongoing contacts.

The reauthorization process offers similar opportunities, but the time available for presenting information is more condensed. Moreover, policy parameters are constrained by existing legislation, and there is likely to be less time to establish credibility. The budget and appropriations processes demand that evaluators monitor the flow of events more closely. Information may need to be stated succinctly and will often need to be tailored to meet specific circumstances. The rush of partisan and program interests in this process is likely to create a search for supporting information, rather than a balanced presentation of evidence. Congressional staffers rely more and more on information from reliable people and organizations, rather than from original sources.

Oversight hearings provide excellent opportunities to present evaluation findings. As the congressional staff interviewees indicated, one must be sure of the intent of a hearing. It may be seeking new information, but it may also be a partisan effort designed to attack and discredit the executive branch, or it may be a symbolic event staged to placate special-interest groups. Knowing the context can guide evaluators' choice of role. Congressionally mandated evaluations provide a unique opportunity to influence the policy process, but these are usually funded and managed by the executive branch, and an interested evaluator needs to work effectively with the administration and with Congress. Radin (1984) provides an interesting and insightful review of evaluations mandated for federal education policy and identified contextual factors that seem to influence the use of such evaluations.

The congressional staff directors reported that effective evaluators produce professional, relevant, and credible information, and develop a network of contacts with congressional staff on both sides of the aisle. In this sense, evaluators are not just providers of facts; rather, they try to influence legislative outcomes in ways consistent with the results of their studies. In many cases, evaluators may work most effectively through intermediate organizations that have established relationships with the legislature and are present to monitor and follow the congressional policy process.

This perspective seems to be consistent with much of what has been observed by others. Lindbloom and Cohen (1979) refer to problem-solving interactions as being key to "professional social inquiry." The same perspective is seen in Young and Comtois's (1979) discussion of congressional uses of evaluation. Young and Comtois note that evaluation must be focused on use, but that the criteria for its relevance are relative rather than absolute. An important factor in the use of evaluation is therefore the interactive process between decision makers and evaluators.

Evaluation—as well as most, if not all, policy analysis—has an important subjective element. One might say that evaluation provides credible support to policy or political arguments. This fact is intuitively understood by politicians and administrators alike. It is necessary for evaluators to acknowledge the normative aspect of policy development in the design, conduct, and presentation of an evaluation. Evaluators cannot, however, ultimately control how their work will be used, and by whom. Legislative decision processes are guided by ideology, as well as by data, and they are generally the products of bargaining rather than of purely rational analysis. This is perhaps most evident in the legislative environment, but one could argue that a similar decision-making dynamic exists in all environments where public policy is addressed.

References

Lindbloom, C. E., and Cohen, D. K. *Usable Knowledge*. New Haven, Conn.: Yale University Press, 1979.
Radin, B. A. "Evaluation on Demand: Two Congressionally Mandated Education Evaluations." In G. R. Gilbert (ed.), *Making and Managing Policy*. New York: Marcel Dekker, 1984.
Weiss, C. H. "Congressional Committee Staffs (Do, Do Not) Use Analysis." In M. Bulmer (ed.), *Social Science Research and Government*. Cambridge, Mass.: Cambridge University Press, 1987.
Young, C. Y., and Comtois, J. "Increasing Congressional Utilization of Evaluation." In F. M. Zweig, *Evaluation In Legislation*. Newbury Park, Calif.: Sage, 1979.
Zweig, F. M. *Evaluation in Legislation*. Newbury Park, Calif.: Sage, 1979.

Michael E. Fishman is director of income assistance policy in the Office of Planning and Evaluation of the U.S. Department of Health and Human Services. He holds an M.A. degree in psychology from Antioch College and is a doctoral student in public administration at the Washington Public Affairs Center of the University of Southern California.

This case study describes an effective team effort and offers perspectives on the short- and long-term impacts of the approach.

Increasing Client Involvement in Evaluation: A Team Approach

Christopher G. Wye

Evaluators are increasingly aware of the desirability of client involvement in the evaluation process. Client involvement can ease communication, facilitate management, and increase credibility. In the process, organizational and functional boundaries between evaluators and program managers may be softened, and a better climate for presenting, discussing, and implementing findings may be established. This chapter describes and assesses an evaluation that incorporated a strategy for maximizing client involvement, with the specific purpose of increasing the utilization of evaluation findings through study teams made up of evaluators and program office staff.

The evaluation was conducted in the Office of Program Analysis and Evaluation (OPAE), within the office of the assistant secretary for Policy Development and Research (PDR) of the U.S. Department of Housing and Urban Development (HUD) in Washington, D.C. The office has a professional staff of about thirty people and a budget for outside services of about $1.5 million. The professional staff is multi-disciplinary: most members have master's degrees, and about half hold the Ph.D. The budget is used mainly to purchase specialized skills and services. Almost all evaluation design, management, and analysis is done by the staff.

The office is frequently called on to perform short-term studies with deadlines of thirty, forty-five, and sixty days. Primarily because of these short-term requests, but also because HUD's in-house data systems are so inadequate, the group almost always collects original data for its studies. This practice has led to the frequent use of phone and mail surveys, combined with on-site interviews and case studies.

The primary client for this evaluation was the Office of Insured Multifamily Housing Development (OIMHD), within the office of the assistant secretary for Housing. A secondary client was the congressional committee responsible for the oversight of HUD's programs. The most important of OIMHD's programs provided subsidized housing in apartment-style multifamily projects for persons of low and moderate income. The evaluation presented in this chapter was an assessment of that program.

The evaluation had its inception several months after the 1976 election. Many of these projects were financially strapped. The number in default, assignment, and foreclosure was growing rapidly and raising serious questions for HUD and Congress about the need for additional subsidies to bail out troubled projects. Congress needed to know how many projects were in financial difficulty, how many more were likely to be in financial difficulty in the future, and how much it would cost to bail them out.

The problem was rooted in the previous administration's hasty implementation of the recently enacted Section 8 for new construction of low-income housing. Under this program, HUD encouraged the building of new low-income housing projects by insuring project mortgages. Responding to congressional pressure to get the program operating quickly, HUD had encouraged the production of a large number of projects in a very short time. Almost inevitably, given the emphasis on production, underwriting standards had been loosely applied, and management concerns were downplayed. The result was a large number of projects that quickly showed signs of financial instability. HUD then had to manage a growing number of projects whose mortgages were in default, assignment, or foreclosure. Financially troubled projects appeared all over the country, the press picked up the story, and Congress pressed for remedial action.

Before HUD could propose a remedy, especially one that would involve asking Congress for additional money, there was a need for clear information on the nature and extent of the problem and what it would cost to fix. Because of the rapid implementation of the program, however, record keeping had been inadequate and management information systems had been poorly designed, and so there was not much information available.

OPAE was given responsibility for the issue, with a deadline of forty-five days. Challenging though this assignment appeared, neither its deadline nor its substance seemed out of line with what had become OPAE's routine agenda, since OPAE had done a number of similar rapid-turnaround studies in the previous two years.

Nevertheless, an issue that had been simmering throughout previous studies boiled over early in the planning for this one. This was the issue of client reaction to, use of, and appreciation for high-effort, rapid-turnaround studies. It had been OPAE's experience that evaluation studies—almost regardless of their timeliness, relevance, or quality—tended more often than not to accentuate rather than soften organizational boundaries between evaluators and clients. In short (and assuming an evaluation of good quality), clients tended to seek control of postevaluation activity, in part by ignoring, distancing themselves from, positioning themselves in regard to, or downplaying the role of the evaluators.

OPAE decided to incorporate into the study a deliberate strategy aimed specifically at this problem. In devising this strategy, OPAE made a distinction between what were termed *structural* and *nonstructural* factors underlying the gap between evaluators and clients. Structural factors were seen as aspects of the relationship about which the least could be done. They included differing conceptual approaches, organizational positions, and purposes. Nonstructural factors, such as anxiety, fear, and ego concerns, were felt to be more susceptible to mitigating strategies. OPAE believed that nonstructural factors could be dealt with through improved human relationships and that better relationships would improve communication and understanding. These in turn might improve other facets of the evaluator-client relationship, and the result would be greater appreciation for the evaluation function and its products. The obvious approach to improving human relationships was having evaluators and clients work closely together in such a way that each could not fail to improve its understanding of the other. OPAE had always encouraged a close working relationship with program staff but had never actively tried to incorporate them into an evaluation.

One way to do this emerged quickly from preliminary thinking about past projects. In many of its short-term studies—especially in those involving on-site data collection in as many sections of the country as this study was likely to involve, and in those that had as many management tasks to be carried out simultaneously—OPAE had divided project staff into two- and three-member teams. OPAE saw no better way for evaluators and program staff to get to know one another than having them work together on such teams during every phase of the project, from initial discussion of methodology to management and evaluation activity to the writing of the final report.

This approach was described in a memorandum that was drafted for the secretary's signature to establish a plan for carrying out the study. Since the political context of the issue seemed to require hard data rather than a theoretical model, OPAE recommended an empirically based study but made no mention of the methodology to be used. The purpose of the evaluation was defined as estimating the number of projects and units currently or potentially liable to be in financial difficulty and the current and probable subsidies needed to bail them out. The memorandum also established a complete management structure and staffing plan, naming two coequal chairpersons to a task force that would address the issue. (The chairpersons were the assistant secretaries of Policy Development and Research and of Housing.) The executive in charge of the low-income housing program was given responsibility for drafting a post-study policy document. The head of OPAE would supervise the evaluation, including its estimates of needed subsidies. The plan called for thirteen teams, each made up of one person from the evaluation office and one person from the program office, with all team members listed by name in the memorandum.

Following the issuance of the memorandum from the secretary, a kickoff meeting was held with all parties except the secretary present. The director of OPAE emphasized the need for teamwork and provided the following ground rules aimed specifically at establishing a positive working relationship between evaluation and program staff:

1. Evaluation and program staff would have equal access to the decision-making process. Regular and open plenary meetings would be held several times a week, at which that director of OPAE would hear comments and make decisions in public. While it was clearly established that OPAE, as the office responsible for the evaluation, would make all decisions, it was also emphasized that all viewpoints would be considered.

2. Evaluation and program staff would participate equally in all phases of the evaluation process, from initial methodological discussions to the final report writing. It was emphasized that this did not mean equal access to information about the evaluation but equal participation in the evaluation itself, and that program staff were to be an integral and valued part of the project. They would be essential to the project's success, as much for their analyses, perceptions, and insights as for their program expertise.

3. Evaluation and program staff would have equal opportunity to air their concerns, questions, and opinions. When issues were decided or questions were answered, the director of OPAE would listen to or read any material offered, announce decisions at the same meetings where issues were raised, and explain his decisions. Participants could appeal a decision at one subsequent meeting.

With these ground rules established, such plenary meetings became an important management device for driving the project and forging an improved relationship between the evaluation and program offices. At these meetings, all important analytical and management issues were presented, discussed, and decided in such areas as issue formulation, methodology, site and interview selection, questionnaire development, travel planning, scheduling, and report drafting. Assignments were always given to teams, rather than to individuals, and were given out from and returned to this group. Plenary sessions were also used for such tasks as stuffing questionnaires into envelopes and coding completed questionnaires.

These meetings also became an important mechanism for forging a more positive relationship between the two functions. The openness of the decision-making process, initially regarded with skepticism, became a source of cohesion as evaluation and program staff increasingly engaged in dialogue and saw their questions, issues, and suggestions openly addressed. Each group gained greater appreciation of the other. Evaluators got a better feel for the political issues faced by administrators, program staff got an improved sense of the methodological issues facing evaluators, and each group gained understanding of the other's management environment.

This latter point was of considerable interest to OPAE. While the evaluation office certainly did not know all there was to know about the internal management of the program office, it still knew something about it, both from similar experience in the past and from its initial experience with the program office. The program staff, however, clearly had no sense of the management or analytical side of evaluation. Their only images of evaluators were based on pejorative adjectives such as *analysts, researchers,* and *academics.* That evaluators might have to do real work to accomplish an evaluation—report to bosses, meet deadlines, accomplish goals, overcome obstacles, solve relationship problems—was something few program staffers had thought about. Improvement in the relationship did not come overnight, however. It occurred over the course of the project and through three fairly distinct stages that roughly coincided with the phases of the study: conceptualization and survey design, data collection and field work, and analysis and write up. The initial phase was marked by the gradual dissolution of overt hostility on the part of program staff and the emergence of their respect for if nothing else, the sheer physical effort required to launch the study. In the early stages of the project, the behavior of program staff at meetings (when they bothered to attend at all) was characterized by tardiness, inattention, and an overall lack of respect for evaluation that was manifested in slouching, turning away from the head of the conference table, and talking during presentations. A marked breakthrough took place at the meeting where the study's methodology and research instruments were established.

The director of OPAE began that meeting by explaining that program records and information systems had been poorly devised and maintained, and that the intense level of congressional interest would demand a high-quality study. Therefore, the only choice was for the project to collect its own data, even if that task added enormous pressure. In another situation, he said, there might have been more latitude to use existing data, perhaps to develop a theoretical model. In this situation, however, the politics of the issue required an approach that would be simple to understand and would provide definitive answers. He recommended, therefore, that the study be designed to include a comprehensive inventory of problems and their costs. In effect, this inventory would constitute a complete management information system retrospectively. This inventory would take the form of a detailed mailout, largely closed ended survey instrument to be filled out by HUD program administrators, local public housing authorities, and professional housing inspectors. The heart of this strategy was to create, by polling the best available expert opinion, a management information system where none had existed. The mailout inventory would be supplemented by in-depth, on-site case studies in selected cities, which would take a closer look at specific troubled projects through the eyes of HUD administrators, Public Housing Authority staff, tenants, cognizant city officials, and other expert groups. The survey instrument would provide a broad statistical picture, and the in-depth case studies would set that picture in motion by showing the underlying dynamics. Moreover, the case studies would be carefully chosen to illustrate the major kinds of situations that had led to financial distress.

The initial reaction of program staff to this proposal was a mixture of incredulity and hostility. This meeting provided the first chance for program staff to ventilate their displeasure with their essentially coerced participation in the study, and a lot of negative emotion came to the surface during the early part of the discussion. There was also a good deal of plain old antipathy: "What good will it do?" "The report will never be read." "It won't be done on time." Many reacted against the idea of a survey, on the grounds that surveys only get opinions, and opinions are not facts. The strongest reaction was that even if a survey was appropriate, one of this complexity would be impossible to do in the time available. This view remained through much of the initial phase of the study.

As time passed, program staffers became more accepting of the methodology but expressed no enthusiasm and retained considerable skepticism. They found it easiest to accept the notion that a modeling or theoretical approach would not be effective in the political environment of the assignment, and hardest to accept the idea that a survey could provide hard data. That an expert opinion is an empirical fact, and that such facts can be aggregated to provide statistical results, was difficult for them to grasp. No one, however, could offer an alternative. The ideal solution, everyone agreed, was a project-by-project audit by a professional firm, but there was not enough time even to draw up a contract, let alone do the audits.

At the end of this meeting, it seemed that program staff had a much better sense of what could not be done than what could be done. Over the next several meetings, however, as the group worked to produce a draft survey instrument, understanding grew. Evaluation staff handled the drafting process as a series of brainstorming sessions. First, the group brainstormed the major generic categories of issues affecting the project's viability, such as design and site, physical structure, and administration. Then each of these issues was taken up individually and subdivided (again, through brainstorming) into its respective components. Project design, for example, was subdivided into unit mix, defensible space, and physical environment.

What emerged from these sessions was a broad categorization of the major issues and a list of their essential components. From these lists, an analytically oriented survey instrument—ultimately called the project problem inventory—was developed to delineate, categorize, and prioritize the major issues of a given project, in a format that allowed rapid completion, aggregation, and summary. The inventory included a standardized checklist of project problems, an analytical discussion of their dynamics, and a structured format for recommending solutions.

As the survey draft began to take shape, program staff's doubts about the ability of a survey to provide hard data began to lessen. In part, their apprehension was reduced by the fact that the survey was to be filled out by virtually all the categories of knowledgeable people, from project managers to professional auditors. At least, they could see, no clearly appropriate type of professional expert or knowledgeable view was being ignored. Their concern was also lessened because they themselves had essentially drafted the substance, if not the final technical form, of the survey by specifying and defining most of the issues. More than anything else, the actual appearance of the first typed version of the survey, organized to provide for ratings, rankings, and easy alphanumeric coding, seemed to dispel the mystery of the survey itself.

While drafting the survey, study teams carried out the many chores necessary to designing the evaluation. During this process, an improved relationship between evaluation and program staff on the study teams continued to narrow the distance between the two functions. The intensity of the effort required to design the study—conceptualizing problems, defining issues, assessing methods, gathering primary and secondary data, assembling relevant literature and reports—seemed to startle program staff. Nothing symbolized the eye-opening nature of the experience for program staff more than the marathon work of collating, stapling, envelope stuffing, addressing, and carrying to the post office of the mail survey, which began on a Saturday at 8 A.M. and ended at midnight.

By the time the study design was completed and the survey was mailed, it was clear that program staff were beginning to peek around the edges of their preconceptions about evaluators. The old conceptions were still there, of course. Expectations were still low, and attitudes were still abrasive, but there was also open respect for the amount of work that had been accomplished and for the dedication, aggressiveness, and persistence it had taken from evaluation staff to get it done. Program staff now felt compelled to make a good-faith effort to hold up their end of the project.

In the next stage, when most of the data collection and field work were done, relationships between the two functions improved a bit more. The improvement appeared to be based on continuing growth in respect for the work involved and on the initial appearance of respect for the evaluation methodology and techniques, program expertise and management ability.

The design of the study's methodology and survey instruments gave program staff a first look at the conceptual side of evaluation. The collection of data and the field work introduced them to the management side. What they saw surprised them. As the study teams prepared to leave for the field, they juggled numerous administrative tasks simultaneously and completed all the necessary and complex arrangements in a week. This included phoning and scheduling interviews with local housing officials and experts, identifying and scheduling visits to troubled housing projects, establishing and coordinating contact with HUD regional and area offices, arranging for travel by plane, limo, car, and public transportation, and making hotel reservations.

All this energy, persistence, and dogged work caught program staff by surprise and gave them a very different view of evaluation. They found the pace, intensity, and complexity of the activity unnerving, especially since the final stages of survey drafting and mailing were simultaneous with the completion of arrangements for travel and field work. Here were no fuzzy-headed bespectacled academics drafting ethereal prose; here was unpleasant, slogging, draining work. Some program staff remarked that, for them, the only equivalent was the launching of a new program, with its cacophony of deadlines, spotlights, and pressures from Congress, reporters, administrators, and clients.

The worst still lay ahead, however, for the intensity of the effort reached its peak during the field work. In five days, thirteen two-person study teams conducted seventy-one interviews, which frequently involved many subjects, and constructed sixty-seven detailed on-site case studies, each of which included a complete financial and management history and an analysis by a professional appraiser. Simultaneously in each city, the study teams oversaw the completion of more than three hundred problem inventories in local HUD offices. By the end of the work week, each team had completed six interviews, six detailed case studies, and twenty-six problem inventories. It was later remarked by a number of team participants that, for program staff, the week of field work was a blur of activity: up early Monday morning, taxi to the airport, plane, limo to hotel, pick up rental car, find way to interview sessions, interview, find way to project for site visit, meet local appraiser and conduct case study and financial analysis, return to HUD office to oversee project inventory surveys, have dinner, work in hotel room clarifying and elaborating notes taken and information gathered during the day, resolve inevitable scheduling mishaps and other unforeseen problems—every day for five days.

As a practical matter, almost all the on-site work was done by the evaluation staff. At this point, program staff wanted to do a full share of the work, but their inexperience with this kind of field work limited their ability to help with scheduling, phoning, traveling, meeting, and dealing with the unexpected. They did help by answering detailed program-related questions concerning the problem inventory, and some focused mainly on this activity, leaving the evaluation staff to handle interviews and site visits.

Program staff were least helpful in the formal interview sessions. In general, their presence made it hard for evaluators to keep subjects focused on the interview questionnaire, complete interviews in the allotted time, and follow up on issues that obviously required more explanation. Although program staffers had been given rudimentary training in interview procedures, their inexperience showed. They had little feel for the amount of time needed to complete the survey documents. They repeatedly took a more informal, conversational approach, which often led to digression, loss of control over the interview, and failure to complete survey documents.

As evaluation staff were forced to assert themselves to maintain control and complete the survey instruments, and as program staff gained a better sense of the techniques and skills needed for a good interview, program staff developed respect for the ability of the evaluation staff to conduct interviews and for the substance of the interviews themselves. Later, when the teams returned to the central office, and later still, after the study had been completed, program staff openly acknowledged their respect for the interview process. The evaluation staff thought that the most important conceptual and interpersonal breakthrough made during the study came in regard to the interview process.

For program staff, the on-site experience had changed their conception of the interview process from one in which they had seen the evaluator as a meddlesome, academic gumshoe collecting gossip in informal, off-the-record conversations aimed at digging up dirt to one in which they saw the evaluator as a dedicated professional gathering data in a highly structured, rigidly disciplined, on-the-record effort intended to establish a true picture of program operations. Program staffers commented on the effort of the evaluation staff to clarify, elaborate on, and verify remarks made during the interview process. They were especially impressed with the evaluator's efforts to maintain a professional rather than a personal relationship with the interview subject. If anything, program staff came to feel that evaluation interviews were overly clinical, but this perception was certainly an improvement over what had been their preconceptions.

Perhaps nothing was of greater surprise to program staff than what the evaluation staff did in the evenings. If there was one aspect of the field work that program staff had anticipated with some enthusiasm, it was the free time that the evenings offered to sample new cities. They were surprised to see evaluation staffers excuse themselves from social activities, in favor of a night in their rooms preparing for the next day's work, and even more surprised at breakfast to find out what this preparation had involved: reviewing survey questionnaires for missing data and incorrect answers, clarifying and elaborating on interview notes, and jotting down insights and tentative conclusions.

Over the course of the week, it became clear that the balances of power (for lack of a better word), if not the balance of energy and expertise, had shifted markedly toward the evaluation function. By the end of the first day, program staffers were jarred by the intensity of the activity and unsure of what role they could play. By the end of the second day, they had conceded de facto leadership in the field work to the evaluation staff and settled into the role of lending their program expertise when it was needed. Thus, there was a single point during the study when program staffers let down their defenses and opened their minds to a reassessment of the evaluation process, it was during the field work. This outcome was partly due to the camaraderie of exhaustion, partly to the inevitable bonding of new friendships, and partly to the program staff's actually seeing and understanding in a new way who evaluators are and what they do.

In the last phase of the study, which involved data preparation, analysis, writeup, and presentation, the relationship between the evaluation and program staffs improved even more and reached its highest point. Although upon their return from the field to the central office organizational lines between the two functions began once more to stiffen as the project moved toward its conclusion, the relationship between the two staffs had significantly changed for the better. Although the resurgence of organizational self-interest was expected, it was especially noticeable in the context of the emotional bonding that had taken place during the field work, when the program and evaluation staffs had worked together under the pressure of tight deadlines and in the intimate structure of two-person teams. Friendships had developed. Viewpoints were shared. Concerns and fears were expressed. At a minimum, program staff now saw evaluation staff as individual human beings rather than as stereotyped abstractions. Now, back from the field, program staffers were clearly defining their roles in the context of their organizational base, as were, it should be noted, evaluation staffers. The evaluation staff showed about the same combination of attitudes—increased emotional attachment to individual program staffers, but a reserved awareness of their own organizational responsibilities. Understandably, each side was anticipating the end of the study and its potentially divergent organizational imperatives.

Renewed organizational concern appeared in a number of settings. On the part of the evaluation staff, it took the form of concern about who would take the lead in formulating analytical conclusions. On the part of the program staff, it took the form of concern about who would take the lead in formulating policy recommendations. On the part of both, it was evident in a reduction in the spontaneity of communication and in greater circumspection on issues vested with organizational implications. It is especially noteworthy that what might be called the general reserve now being expressed by program staff appeared to originate less with those who had participated in the field work than with their supervisors and colleagues who had stayed behind. It seemed clear to the evaluation staff that the program staff was reflecting signals from its own chain of command, among which the most powerful seemed to be fear of the evaluation itself.

Much later, when the study was long over, it became clear that during this period a minidrama had been unfolding within the program office around its organizational posture toward the evaluation office. Program staff had returned from the field impressed with the evaluation staff, and they shared their views with their superiors. The immediate results in the program office were a significant increase in fear at high executive levels and a signal to the program staff to be careful. This fear emerged even though evaluation and program executives had been meeting on almost a daily basis during the study, as a part of the overall client-oriented strategy developed by OPAE.

Nevertheless, despite the pressures exerted by their superiors, program staff made it clear that they were in the study for the duration, and they made a conscientious effort to hold up their end during the final stages. In general, their contributions were more useful in data preparation than in analysis and writing. At this point, everyone was tired, but program staffers, for whom the newness of the experience constituted an extra burden, were especially weary. Although they were careful to carry out their assignments—coding and checking surveys, assembling and arraying data—even in these relatively mechanical tasks they missed deadlines, and higher-than-normal error rates were frequent.

With respect to the analytical aspects of the project, especially those involving quantitative methodology, program staff obviously felt out of place, and they said so. By this point, they had come to trust the judgment of the evaluation staff enough to respect reasonably sophisticated quantitative methodological techniques, rather than dismissing them as intellectual mumbo-jumbo. Nevertheless, they felt unequipped to participate in this work. Many efforts were made to encourage their participation and develop their understanding, but without much success. One sensed, underneath, a certain lack of interest.

Nonquantitative analytical work elicited a higher (but still modest) level of interest and participation. This facet of the study was handled in a series of open meetings, with individual analysts presenting case studies on specific projects, after which the group sought to agree on interpretive conclusions. Program staff seemed impressed by the evaluation analysts, who carefully applied rules of evidence, causality, representativeness, and association to the information. Occasionally, program staff would offer insightful comments based on past experience. For the most part, however, they left the analysis to the evaluation staff.

Once the major conclusions were formulated and agreed to in open meeting, specific recommendations for assembly of evidence and writeup were assigned to each study team. The writeup consisted of formulating a series of very short, usually no more than five-line summary statements and drafting supporting text providing related evidence, analyses, and conclusions. Program staff were not helpful in this process. With no training in analytical methods, they were unable to sort through the data with much confidence, and they tended to get bogged down in details. Primarily for this reason, program staff were unable to produce much writing for the final report; almost all of it was done by the evaluation staff.

Program staff were, however, quite helpful in formulating policy recommendations. Once the analytical work was done and the report was written, program staff quickly came to grips with the practical implications of the study. Their contributions to the process of developing recommendations were frequently quick, sharp, insightful, and intuitive, and they often simultaneously accounted for the managerial, political, and personnel dimensions in ways that were at first only barely apparent to the evaluation staff. They knew the ground rules of their own operations as thoroughly as the evaluation staff knew its analytical techniques.

This is not to suggest that the evaluation staff made no contribution to this process, for the evaluation staff conceptualized and led most of the discussion. Once an issue had been laid out, however, contributions from program staffers were spontaneous and incisive. Spirited dialogues frequently arose between the evaluation and program staffs. Of all of the phases of the study, it was during this one that the two staffs worked together most productively on an equal footing. On any given issue, the evaluation staff tended to have the larger view, based on its experience with placing individual pieces of data and analysis into an analytical whole. The program staff had the more incisive recommendations, based on its intimate knowledge of program operations.

Once the report was done and the recommendations were formulated, program staffers performed an invaluable function by generating credibility among their colleagues and superiors. The initial reaction among program executives was fairly typical. They did not expect the study to be accurate, credible, or helpful in the policy process. Behind closed doors, however, program staff who had participated in the study held their own with their superiors, insisting that the study was credible and ought to be considered.

Discussion in the program office continued for several weeks. The primary cleavage was between those who had participated in the study and those who had not. Much later, it was learned that study participants were subjected to considerable pressure—ranging from the hallway quips of colleagues to the implied threats of superiors—regarding their support for the report and especially for the evaluators who had worked on it. Program executives eventually accepted the report and most of its recommendations and expressed unusually respectful appreciation for the evaluation and the evaluation staff. As an unanticipated utilization strategy, which was also another compliment to the evaluation staff, a program official asked OPAE to conduct a flip-chart briefing for congressional committee staff as a way of building credibility for HUD's proposed response to the "troubled projects" problem. HUD proposed and Congress later approved the exact subsidy amount suggested by the evaluation study.

Another unanticipated consequence of this study was that it virtually made the reputation of the OPAE evaluation function with the assistant secretary for Housing and his executive staff. From that point on, the assistant secretary for PDR received an increasing number of requests for analytical work that specifically asked for the services of OPAE. A year after the initial study, the assistant secretary for Housing had made so many requests that OPAE could not handle them all, and the assistant secretary for PDR began to meet with the assistant secretary for Housing on a regular basis, to set priorities for the studies that could be done. Ultimately, the assistant secretary for Housing made a formal request to have OPAE transferred to his operation—a request that was quickly declined, but with appreciation.

This evaluation experience was unusually successful in bringing evaluation and program staffs closer together, with the specific purpose of increasing client use of the evaluation. The theory tested through this exercise—that if each party to the evaluation knew more about the other, improved human relationships would follow, including the development of mutual understanding, respect, and good will—proved correct in this situation, and it should lead to similar outcomes in other situations. The key elements of this transformation were the joint participation of the evaluation and program staffs at all stages and the openness of the work process. Had program staff been permitted to participate on a part-time basis and to avoid such experiences as intense pressure at the evaluation core or the professionalism of the interview process, their participation would have lost some of its most important meaning. Moreover, had program staffers not been able to participate in all aspects of the evaluation, especially decision making, they probably would have harbored doubts about those parts of the evaluation they had not participated in, and those doubts might have distorted their total image of the evaluation.

Christopher G. Wye is director of the Office of Program Analysis and Evaluation in the Office of Community Planning and Development at the U.S. Department of Housing and Urban Development. He holds M.A. and Ph.D. degrees in history and political science from Kent State University and presidential rank in the Senior Executive Service.

Team planning meetings, frequent briefings, and program reviews leading to action plans are techniques that can work in international and domestic settings.

Three Techniques for Helping International Program Managers Use Evaluation Findings

Robert Werge, Richard A. Haag

This chapter presents three techniques for evaluating international development programs more effectively, in terms of the needs of program managers. All three techniques involve the evaluator's assuming the role of facilitators who can, on the one hand, identify and clarify information needs and, on the other, communicate findings to address those needs. The facilitator role is important in both the domestic and the international context because it implies that evaluators have assumed a crosscultural perspective in their work. In domestic and international situations alike, program managers and evaluators frequently say that they feel like strangers in a strange land, where each party seems to be speaking a language unintelligible to the other.

Two of the techniques, team planning meetings and frequent briefings, employ organizational development methods applied to short-term evaluation missions. The third, a program review process, is directly related to the internal function that evaluation can play in international organizations.

The dramatic cross-cultural nature of international evaluation has heightened the present authors' awareness of crucial factors in the relationship between evaluators and program managers. These factors intensify the problem of communicating the critical assumptions, needs, and expectations involved in evaluation. The design and conduct of international evaluations must take the following factors into account:
- The diverse geographical, cultural, linguistic, and political systems across which program managers operate
- The highly decentralized day-to-day operations that affect program objectives, methods, requirements, and procedures
- The high value often placed on oral and personal communication in a "host" language
- Extremely heterogeneous clients and organizational cultures, with distinct viewpoints on the meaning and politics of evaluation.

Clearly, such factors also affect domestic evaluations, underscoring the need for evaluators everywhere to pay much closer attention to their facilitation skills. These skills can be as crucial as evaluators' traditional methodological skills. For example, on a recent mission to India, several U.S. range-management evaluators conducted an assessment of current practices in the Rajasthan Desert area and developed a series of recommendations for more rational livestock control. Their evaluation, however, overlooked the fact that in India cattle are sacred and have important symbolic meaning for their owners and for the governments of Rajasthan and India. Livestock program managers in India take into account a much broader range of religious, economic, and ecological factors than their counterparts do in the United States. Policy and program decisions must reflect these broader concerns.

In an international context, the evaluator must be extremely sensitive to cultural factors that affect how program managers define their goals and their success, and evaluators must employ techniques that incorporate these factors into the overall evaluation design. Such techniques can also be important in a domestic context. The three communication and training techniques described in this chapter have been used by the authors to establish an "incorporative" and "facilitating" approach to evaluation.

Team Planning Meetings (TPMs)

Short-term international evaluation teams are often composed of staff members and consultants brought together by international agencies to assess overseas projects or programs. Members of the team are expected to work together under intense constraints imposed by time, physical discomfort, cultural differences, and uncertainty. Members often have not worked together before and represent different disciplines and combinations of skills.

TPMs use human resources training to improve the effectiveness of short-term international expert teams. This method was first used by an agency of the U.S. Department of Agriculture, the Office of International Cooperation and Development, and has been modified by other groups, most notably the Water and Sanitation for Health Project, based in Arlington, Virginia (Gormley and Rosenweig, 1985; Kettering, 1988). This approach is well suited to international program managers, who need to develop evaluation teams with sustained ability to solve conceptual, methodological, and logistical problems in the field. It allows the team to keep track of overall evaluation goals and objectives.

The TPM process offers a set of training exercises, paced over a one- or two-day period, before the team begins its work overseas. TPMs allow a team to clarify its objectives and methods by reviewing individual members' expectations, resources, skills, and work strategies. The training exercises are usually conducted by a trainer who is neutral in terms of the program or project being evaluated and who helps the team leader, team members, and the program manager to work toward common understanding of the evaluation's goals and objectives. A successful TPM process results in an implementation strategy based on specific schedules, priorities, and divisions of responsibility. Most important, it defines roles, so that team members can make periodic adjustments in the evaluation process as information is collected and in-country client needs become clear.

In typical TPMs facilitators structure the following activities:
1. Sharing of team members' backgrounds, experience, and expectations (Who comes from where? Who has what specialty? Who has worked in the country before?)
2. Clarifying expectations and resources for logistical and other support (How much is the per diem allowance? Can cars be rented?)
3. Reviewing the history and politics of the evaluation (Why is this evaluation being done, and why now?)
4. Identifying clients and their perspectives on the evaluation (Who wants the evaluation done? How will the clients use the information?)
5. Reviewing the scope of work and clarifying and setting priorities for its objectives (Which of the areas is the most important? If time becomes more of a constraint, which of the areas can be dropped?)
6. Developing a tentative action plan (In the six days we have in country X, how much time will we spend on site visits versus data collection in the capital? Who will do what?)
7. Agreeing on specific assignments (Who will work with the budget data, and who will collect qualitative case studies?)
8. Establishing guidelines for periodic assessment of the evaluation process and the team's work (Will we meet each Friday to review how well we are working as a team?)

9. Sharing preferences for the use of free time (Who expects to spend the evenings writing? Who needs time for physical exercise?)
10. Reaching agreement on team norms (What are the roles and responsibilities of the team leader going to be?).

Once an open climate for information sharing is established in a TPM, an evaluation team is in a good position to respond to and interpret the program manager's needs as new conditions and circumstances arise in the field. For example, if the evaluation team is producing a report as a final product, the TPM provides an opportunity to develop a rough outline. It may be extremely important, for example, that a team know that the project manager expects a report of approximately sixty single-spaced pages, with several matrices outlining key issues. The proposed length of the report helps evaluators roughly determine the level of qualitative detail required for the report to be useful. A program manager's insistence on a very brief summary (two pages maximum) can also help team members set the level of synthesis required.

In short, the TPM approach can help international program managers clarify their own objectives and expectations, as well as the evaluators', before overseas work begins. TPMs provide a concentrated, structured environment in which clarification can occur, and they allow program managers and evaluators to gain additional perspectives on final outcomes and to reach agreements leading to broad use of an evaluation.

Frequent Briefings with Program Managers

As an evaluation team moves from one country to another, it must be able to identify and understand the concerns and perspectives of overseas program managers. This process is greatly aided by frequent briefings on the team's objectives, progress, and findings.

Oral briefings, as a form of dialogue, complement written reports and documents. In many organizations, there is a substantial gap between the production of written reports and their use by program managers. Managerial decisions are generally made on the basis of information derived from short conversations in groups or in one-to-one meetings. Written reports have important functions, including the documentation and communication of information for formal purposes, but decision making is more often informal. Through briefings, evaluators are often in a better position to influence decisions than if they rely on their reports. For example, during an assessment in Peru, one of the present authors was asked to lead a review team, which was examining socioeconomic research at an international institute, and to synthesize the team's findings in a final report. The report would be presented to a larger panel of about thirty experts and administrators. One disadvantage of having such a large group review a single document, however, is that editorial and stylistic comments become confused with substantive agreement or disagreement.

Therefore, instead of distributing the written report to the larger panel, the author gave an oral briefing of the team's report, using an overhead projector to highlight its findings. This briefing allowed the experts and administrators to focus on the important recommendations of the team and seek greater clarification. They pointed out areas of their agreement and disagreement. Instead of becoming involved in editing or rewriting the report, the experts and administrators focused on its substance and the findings on which they might act. At the end of the briefing, copies of the written report were distributed, and only then were the experts and administrators asked to submit editorial comments and suggestions.

There are at least three critical junctures where evaluators can effectively use briefings to maximize the impact of their work during short-term studies. The first is at the beginning of an investigation, to clarify objectives and methods with program managers. If a TPM process has been carried out before an evaluation team goes overseas, the team should provide a briefing when it arrives in the host country. This briefing begins an ongoing dialogue with the in-country managers and counterparts who join the team at this point.

A second important juncture appears after the team has completed its field work but has not yet begun to compose its report. The briefing at this point is perhaps the most important one, for it occurs when it is possible for the team to set priorities for its findings, in terms of a manager's main concerns. On many international evaluation teams, what interests the evaluators does not necessarily interest the program managers. A briefing at this time gauges the degree to which the report addresses important issues. For example, a Latin American forestry evaluation team became concerned about a forestry official who was hostile to the aims of the project, but not to the resources it offered. At a briefing before the final report was drafted, the principal administrator said that the official's hostility was political in nature; if it were highlighted in the report, it would jeopardize the project in other regions. The report did mention the situation in passing, without giving it the emphasis that the team originally had planned. The report also included comments on several "hot" issues that the program manager had raised. These would not have been mentioned in the report otherwise.

A third juncture where briefings are critical comes after the report is finished. As already noted, oral briefings can have an impact beyond that of written reports because they fit into the informal decision-making process that characterizes many international organizations. An open, oral presentation, combined with questions and answers, can engage a range of managers and begin a dialogue among them and with the evaluation team on the implications of a particular assessment. The final written report of the team becomes a reference tool, which is reviewed to reinforce the findings that have already been heard.

Program Reviews to Produce Action Plans

The third technique for improving the effectiveness of an evaluation is to link its findings to the program manager's planning and budget functions. This step requires evaluators to initiate a planning process of their own that is based on their findings. Most international program managers are responsible for developing action plans that specify what they will do to reach their goals and objectives. They must also develop detailed annual and operating budgets, showing what resources they need. Evaluation results are more likely to be seen as useful when they provide meaningful information that can be used for program and budget decisions. From this perspective, evaluation systems need to measure what happens when plans and budgets are implemented, by documenting actual activities and outcomes (rather than planned activities and intended outcomes). Without such measurement, there is no real feedback among plans, budgets, and results. Thus, evaluation results can be used to demonstrate that the things planned and budgeted were implemented and had the intended results (effects, outcomes, or impacts).

Since 1981, the Peace Corps has been experimenting with a "country program review" (CPR) process to help meet the Peace Corps' need for better management information (Haag, 1984). Headquarters evaluation staffers used four principles to developing the CPR process. First, the process had to provide results that could be seen by the staff as helping with the programming, training, and support functions of volunteers. Second, key people, especially host sponsors and ministry officials, had to have meaningful roles in the process. Third, Washington support staffers and senior managers had to be able to use the summarized information. Fourth, the process had to generate a set of standardized instruments and procedures that could be used to monitor Peace Corps posts anywhere.

The CPR process involves a Peace Corps evaluation staff person helping in-country staffers and volunteers collect information from a number of crucial actors in the Peace Corps' daily operations. (A CPR survey in Central America, for instance, involved over 350 Peace Corps and host people as respondents; staffers and volunteers used short questionnaires, structured interviews, and observation checklists, all of which they reviewed and approved beforehand.) In the CPR process, a host consultant is also hired to interview a broad segment of host officals with whom staffers work. Survey results are tallied and summarized by the evaluator. Staff and volunteer representatives then have an all-day retreat, facilitated by the evaluator, to review and interpret results and draft an action plan that outlines specific steps for improving the overall program. This plan is then shown to other Peace Corps staffers, as well as to key host officials. Staffers and volunteers also review and update plans periodically, to document progress.

The CPR focuses on issues (highlighted by evaluation results) that program managers say they want and need to know about. All the key participants in a Peace Corps program overseas (volunteers, staffers, host sponsors, and ministry officials) are asked how programs are being managed and whether projects and volunteers are accomplishing their goals. The results help managers to check on whether the things planned have been achieved and to see where they can improve programming, training, and support. The results also help senior managers explain to host sponsors and officials (as well as to U.S. taxpayers) what the Peace Corps is doing, and how well.

The Peace Corps staff and volunteers have been most responsive to the CPR process. They believe it does provide useful information to help improve training, programs, and support. Moreover, they say that the process may be as important as the results. The CPR instruments and procedures stimulate communication and scrutiny, providing a consistent, objective format for summarizing, analyzing, and interpreting information. Managers especially like the action plans, because staffers and volunteers jointly develop them and provide follow-up tracking to show what future actions have occurred. They feel that these are their own plans, not plans inherited from visiting experts. (Evaluators refer to themselves as technical consultants and group facilitators commissioned by the staff and volunteers to help them reach their own goals.)

Thus, action plans are the keys to the CPR process. These brief plans are anchored in real management operations. They are also specific. They identify key issues, list recommended steps to deal with each issue, indicate who is responsible for carrying out each step, and provide estimated schedules for accomplishing each step. Because these action plans have been developed in, by, and for the field, they become working documents meant to be shared with others in the country (as well as at headquarters). They are updated periodically by the people who developed them.

The staff and volunteers especially appreciate having written, concise plans against which actual accomplishments can be measured over time. A major complaint against traditional evaluations is the tendency for lengthy reports to be forgotten or buried. Action plans, in contrast, are meant to be reviewed and updated. Action plans thus address a common lament: "We talked endlessly about what needed to be done, but then nothing ever happened, and we never heard why."

Conclusion

This chapter has focused on three techniques that international evaluators find useful for facilitating dialogue with program managers. The first two techniques, team planning meetings and frequent briefings, increase the clarity with which evaluators and managers communicate on objectives, methods, and priorities. Both techniques are designed to guide short-term evaluation teams (while the teams, under great pressure in unfamiliar environments, help managers improve their programs through assessment). The third technique, program reviews that produce action plans, is designed to help evaluators work with managers to make structural connections with planning and budgeting procedures. This technique addresses the problem of incorporating evaluation into program managers' planning and budget responsibilities.

The context in which these techniques have been presented is that of international agencies, but the organizational environment of domestic agencies is also sufficiently cross-cultural to respond to these techniques. The development of evaluators' facilitation skills—in planning evaluations, conducting briefings, and integrating findings into action plans—can be crucial to the successful use of evaluation results. The authors hope that more experience with these techniques, in the United States and abroad, will increase the chances of effective interaction between evaluators and program managers.

References

Gormley, W., and Rosenweig, F. *Facilitator's Guide for Conducting a Team Planning Meeting*. Water and Sanitation for Health Project technical report, no. 32. Washington, D.C.: Office of Health, Bureau of Science and Technology, U.S. Agency for International Development, 1985.

Haag, R. *Country Program Review Monitoring: A Field Manual*. Washington, D.C.: Office of Planning, Assessment, and Management Information, U.S. Peace Corps, October 1984.

Kettering, M. *Making Technical Assistance Teams More Effective*. (Rev. ed.) Washington, D.C.: Development Program Management Center, Technical Assistance Division, Office of International Cooperation and Development, U.S. Department of Agriculture, 1988.

Robert Werge is a consultant in planning and evaluation. His most recent federal position was director of the Office of Planning and Policy Analysis at the Peace Corps. He holds a Ph.D. in anthropology from the University of Florida.

Richard A. Haag is a management analyst with Peace Corps' Office of Planning and Policy Analysis. He has been on Peace Corps staff in Fiji and Afghanistan and has done evaluation work in over a dozen countries. He holds a Ph.D. in psychology from the University of Hawaii.

A collaborative approach to evaluation is aided by program managers' ability to determine their own readiness and the readiness of the evaluators.

Advice for the Evaluated

Joseph N. Coffee

The relationships that develop between decision makers and evaluators cause many of the problems encountered during program evaluation. Poor relationships often develop from lack of agreement on the strategic and tactical process dimensions of the evaluation. These dimensions range from the purpose of the evaluation and how it will be conducted to how the findings will be presented. This lack of agreement—or, often, failure even to discuss the issues underlying a decision maker's concerns—leads to suspicion about motives and, eventually, to an evaluation that lacks the kind of credibility and positive impact it could have had.

This chapter is written from the perspective of an organizational development consultant providing guidance, support, and suggestions to a program manager wanting to (or having to) work effectively with evaluators. I have chosen to present this material from this perspective for several reasons. First, many of the concerns and frustrations described by career executives and political appointees are amenable to this type of treatment. Second, my experience in conducting organizational development interventions in other settings is relevant. Finally, it will probably be informative and helpful for evaluators to hear these issues presented from their clients' perspective. With respect to the last point, some of the techniques and actions described in this chapter were mentioned by executives and political appointees. This is not surprising, since these techniques are widely taught in formal courses and are frequently developed through trial and error. The suggestions presented to program managers (a term I use for both career and appointed line managers) are offered with the assumption that an evaluation is imminent and inevitable. This "here and now" perspective is used to keep the advice pragmatic. As one wag observed, "An imminent hanging tends to focus one's attention."

Advice to the Program Manager

Your program responsibility brings you in contact with many organizations besides your own. Over time, a "family" of interorganizational relationships develops. Many program managers spend much of their energy assessing and attempting to influence this family of relationships, because these are often crucial to the achievement of a program's goals.

From time to time, you will probably experience an addition to this family of relationships: an interorganizational relationship with an evaluation staff. This new relationship may not be something you would have chosen, but it is something that most public managers expect, given the nature of programs and resources. We all recognize that we are accountable to the public (although it would simply be less frightening and disruptive if we were permitted to make our own assessments of our programs' performance). Figure 1 provides an abbreviated schematic presentation of a family of interorganizational relationships experienced by a typical federal manager. It demonstrates how relationships are compounded by the addition of a single party—an evaluation staff, for example.

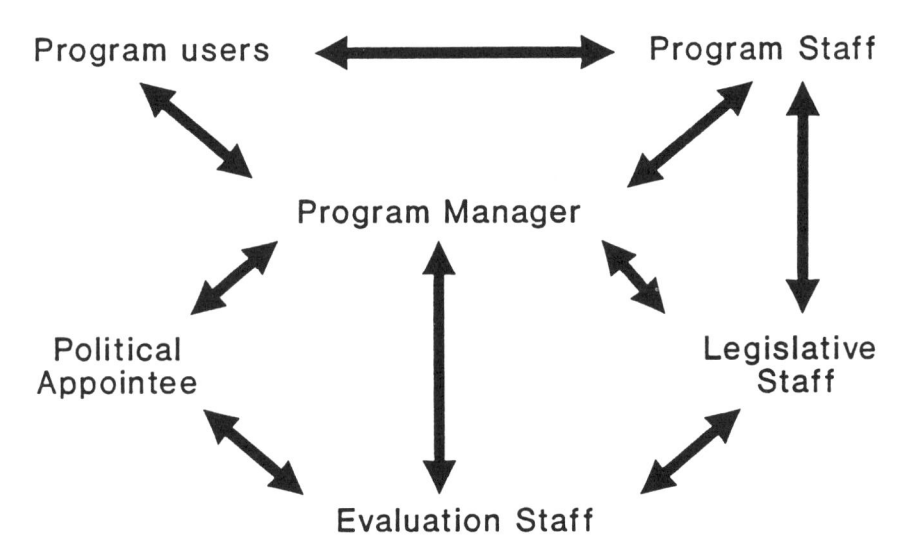

Figure 1. Interorganizational Relationships

Several factors may make the relationship with an evaluation staff problematic. The relationship is frequently sporadic or intermittent, so that you have little prior knowledge of the staff members. The arrival of an evaluation staff is frequently a sign that someone is concerned about the effectiveness or efficiency of your program. Moreover, evaluation staffs are frequently given little time to complete their work, and time pressure increases for all parties.

Many program managers assume the worst. They assume that the evaluators are mean-spirited, politically motivated, rewarded only for finding out what is wrong, and unable (because they lack interest, ability, or time) to learn about the challenges that program managers face. There are evaluators and evaluation staffs who exhibit all those characteristics, and the ideas, suggestions, and techniques presented in this chapter are not meant to persuade you that evaluators should not be viewed with initial suspicion. Rather, they are presented in the expectation of your discovering that evaluators, like everyone else, display a mixture of characteristics. The material in this chapter will help you determine the nature of the evaluation staff and influence your relationship with this staff in the way that will be most beneficial to you. This chapter provides techniques and tools for scanning the important characteristics of an evaluation staff and offers guidance for dealing with the evaluation staff after such scanning.

Evaluating the Evaluators

There are three steps that you, as a manager, can take to assess evaluators before you decide how to deal with a proposed evaluation. Step 1 is a general scan of the situation. It will help you decide whether you have or can get the information you need. Step 2 is a detailed scan of the situation, consisting largely of data collection. Step 3 is the final scan, which includes classifying the evaluator and the situation into one of four common categories. Here, you decide the level of your readiness (which in turn may decide the level at which the evaluation staff will operate). The results of this classification will strongly determine the appropriate course of action.

Step 1: General Scan. As a manager, you need to have basic information about an impending evaluation, to begin making a reasonable assessment of the impact it may have on your programs. To get this information, you must ask yourself the following types of questions:
- Do I have a fairly good idea of the purpose of the evaluation?
- Do I know whom the evaluator considers to be the client?
- If my concerns can be worked out, can the results of the evaluation be useful to my program? Can I be a client?
- Do I know who will conduct the evaluation?

- Am I aware of the evaluation leader's interpersonal and technical skills?
- Am I aware of the evaluation staff's interpersonal and technical skills?

These are areas that should be touched on in initial communications between you and the evaluation leader. They can be answered directly and are reasonable questions that an experienced evaluator will expect. In fact, one early measure of evaluators' experience and sensitivity is the extent to which they actively seek to share this kind of information with you. If the evaluators are initially unknown or unavailable to you, this information should be sought from any possible source.

When you do not know the answers to these questions, it is reasonable to feel anxious about and protective of your program. Knowing the answers provides a good base for you to begin making decisions about how to treat the evaluation effort. Moreover, you must know the answers before you can go on to Step 2.

Step 2: Detailed Scan. Managers, at any given time before or during a specific evaluation, have a certain readiness for personal and organizational involvement. Readiness is based on your expectations (both positive and negative) for how the evaluation results will be used, your perception of the evaluators' interpersonal and interorganizational skills, and your perception of the evaluators' technical competence and understanding of the crucial aspects of your program.

Nine questions need to be answered as soon as possible after your relationship with the evaluators has begun to develop. Many are related to activities that may not come until much later, but you should get the answers quickly, while you still have an opportunity to make changes.

1. Will the evaluation staff have reasonably minimal demands on the time and energy of my staff?
2. Will the evaluation focus on portions of the program that are important to us?
3. Do I know and feel comfortable with the evaluation process?
4. Do I have some power to change the process, and some control over the data developed during the evaluation?
5. Is the evaluation staff willing to be held responsible for the quality of the data and the efficiency of the process?
6. Will the evaluation produce useful results in time for me to use them?
7. Is the evaluation team trying to produce information in tune with our decision-making process and style?
8. Does the evaluation staff know the important characteristics of the program and the program staff?
9. Is the evaluation staff aware of (and willing to shape its results to reflect) the budgetary and legislative realities of the program?

Some of these questions are irrelevant to some programs, and it is appropriate to consider the relevance of each one before you expend any effort on answers. These are also very subjective questions, and no quantitative scoring system is possible. The point here is to suggest specific information that will help you arrive at an informed opinion about an evaluation's possible impact on your program. These questions may also be particularly valuable to the growing number of program managers who have found that evaluations are an effective management tool and an efficient learning technique.

The next eight questions may be more difficult to answer early in the process, since accurate answers may come only through observation, rather than from the evaluation staff itself. Nevertheless, these questions are appropriate.

1. Does the evaluation team have positive negotiation skills (for example, to obtain data that must be supplied by others)?
2. Can the evaluation staff recognize and resolve differences to the satisfaction of all parties?
3. Can and will the evaluation staff help my staff interpret data in a nonthreatening way?
4. Can the evaluation staff recognize and work within the program's political realities and environment?
5. Are members of the evaluation staff willing to work within the program's existing political processes?
6. Do head evaluators (or other recognized members of the evaluation team) demonstrate leadership skills?
7. Do members of the evaluation team have enough self-confidence to suggest changes in the scope, purpose, and focus of the evaluation, on the basis of new information?
8. Can members of the evaluation team share information in a way that promotes understanding and decreases defensiveness?

The final set of questions deals with the technical abilities of the evaluation staff. Evaluators need the analytical skills associated with data collection, manipulation, and presentation. They also must be able to understand the technical dimensions of any program that they are evaluating.

One of the biggest nightmares a program manager can have is to encounter an evaluation staff that does not have the technical ability to handle an evaluation effectively. You may not be able to know whether this is the case until you see the final product, particularly if evaluators combine deficient technical skills with poor interpersonal skills that minimize interaction during evaluation. If you can assess the evaluation staff's technical ability, you will have a much better opportunity to make prompt and effective adjustments.

1. Can the evaluation staff clearly state the program's performance

objectives? (The program staff may need to help with consensus on these objectives.)
2. Does the evaluation staff recognize the difference between what can be measured and what is important?
3. Does the evaluation staff seem able to produce high-quality results in the face of constraints on time and resources?
4. Can members of the evaluation staff package the evaluation results to reflect the needs of various recipients?
5. Can the evaluators demonstrate the relevance of data to the important dimensions of the program?
6. Are members of the evaluation staff willing to describe the weaknesses of their data, findings, and conclusions? Do they automatically include appropriate disclaimers?
7. Do the evaluators demonstrate a variety of data-collection and data-analysis skills, to provide trade-offs among speed, accuracy, and costs?

Step 3: Final Scan. If you have been able to answer many of the questions for Step 2, you can now come to an overall or summative scan of the prospective evaluation. With or without the answers, however, you will no doubt come to some conclusion that will determine how you react to the evaluation staff; seeing the dimensions of the situation, as suggested by the variety of these questions, simply provides an orderly way to proceed.

There are four levels of evaluation readiness (see Figure 2). Determining the level of your own readiness will mean subjectively combining all the information you have collected about the evaluation team and the other important dimensions of the evaluation. Obviously, there are many gradations of these levels, but the purpose of describing your particular situation in these terms is to determine appropriate actions.

Figure 2. Levels of Evaluation Readiness

Level 1	I do not want this evaluation. I see little of value coming from it. I lack confidence in the technical ability of the evaluators, and they do not have enough experience with my type of program.
Level 2	I believe the evaluation could be useful, and the evaluators have the technical and interpersonal skills, but they do not have enough experience with my type of program.
Level 3	I believe the evaluation could be useful, and the evaluators have experience with my type of program, but I lack confidence in their technical or interpersonal skills.
Level 4	I believe the evaluation could be useful. The evaluators have the needed technical and interpersonal skills, and they have sufficient experience with my type of program.

Using the Information

For each level of evaluation readiness, I have made some suggestions. Each situation has unique factors, which will require your judgment and modification of approaches, and so I urge you to be creative in your interpretation and application of these suggestions.

Your perceptions may change as the evaluation progresses, and it may be beneficial to reconsider your perceptions from time to time. Additional information from your staff, peers, superiors, and particularly the evaluation staff may help you refine your judgments.

I have couched these suggestions in positive terms, assuming that all parties want the most effective evaluation and program possible. It is true, however, that evaluators sometimes have to conduct apparently useless or politically motivated evaluations. Managers may believe that they or their programs have everything to lose. A whole array of other reasons and different situations also discourage people from working together with openness and trust.

Suggestions for Level 4. At level 4 of readiness, your primary task is to get on with the evaluation and cement a mutually beneficial relationship with the evaluation staff. You will want to verify your current perceptions and assure members of the evaluation staff that you see the evaluation very positively. You should realize that members of the evaluation staff may also be concerned about the type of relationship they will be able to establish. Positive feedback can ensure that a good situation does not deteriorate for lack of attention. Situations are not always what they appear to be from one point of view, and your early attention to the relationship will provide the information you need to increase your confidence. In encouraging you to take these positive steps, I make several assumptions.

1. You and members of your staff have the same interpersonal skills that you expect the evaluation staff to have.
2. You or your staff have a fairly good idea of areas in which your program could be improved, or at least of areas in which more data would be useful.
3. You have good knowledge of the range of technical skills that the evaluation staff should possess.
4. You believe that evaluations do not need to have winners or losers.

Early meetings with the evaluation staff should result in an agreement or a contract that briefly defines how tasks important to you will be handled.

Suggestions for Level 3. This level of readiness is a good situation. You view the evaluation staff as having the technical and interpersonal skills to interact effectively with you, other decision makers, and the program staff, and you perceive the evaluation as useful for improving

or justifying your program. Your main concern is to help the evaluation staff develop sufficient knowledge of your program area. In most cases, the evaluation staff will also see this task as important and necessary, although differences may evolve over how it is done. For instance, evaluation staff members may believe that they will pick up the necessary program knowledge as they conduct the evaluation. If you want the evaluation staff to describe the real impact of the program (not just its quantifiable data) and ensure that the targets of the evaluation are important to the program mission, you may want another approach. Consider the following:
1. Provide the evaluation staff with written material on the program, possibly including literature disseminated to the public, legislative hearings, speeches, other evaluations, budgets, and reports of accomplishments.
2. Name the program staffers who will be available to answer questions.
3. Ask the evaluators to prepare one or more papers that indicate their thorough understanding of the program, including what its real impact was intended to be, is, or should be; who its key stakeholders are; and the barriers to its being more successful and the elements supporting its success.
4. Meet with the evaluators to discuss their papers. Use the session for the evaluation staff, you, and your staff to learn. The benefit will be insight from previously uninvolved people, which may give you and your staff opportunities to view your program differently. (Program people are often too close to a program to see the obvious.) This interactive session should be nonevaluative; that is, it should focus on the evaluation staff's understanding of the program and on your staff's understanding of the evaluators' perceptions.
5. If there are still areas that the evaluation staff has to understand better, repeat the procedure up to this point, providing additional material and advice.
6. Once you are convinced that the evaluators understand the program well enough, both of you should be at level 4 and can follow that advice to the appropriate extent.

Throughout this process, and at any level, you typically will be trying to establish the conditions that will make you comfortable with the evaluation. Your efforts to help evaluators understand your program, and the process involved in that task, will of course have to be made with a view to other possible concerns. These include the use of your staff's resources and the time requirements for completing the evaluation.

Nevertheless, level 3 is usually relatively easy to negotiate. All evaluators agree that a thorough knowledge of the program is essential. As the program manager, you should have the most control over how that knowledge is imported, and you should have control over the information required for an understanding of your program.

Suggestions for Level 2. In many ways, this is the toughest level. Here, you believe that evaluation would be useful and that the evaluation staff has a good understanding of your program, but you have little confidence in the evaluation staff's technical or interpersonal skills. You realize that the lack of either skill could seriously disrupt or harm your program. Unless the evaluators readily admit deficiencies in one or both of these areas, the evaluation staff will probably be defensive and resist your efforts to deal with your concerns. The following suggestions may help you work with evaluators who fail either to admit or deal with their deficiencies. These suggestions are designed to help solve the problem, whether the deficiencies are caused by technical or interpersonal incompetence or both.

In most cases, you will find that your best chance of managing conflict or potential differences is to begin where there is some agreement or some knowledge in common. In this case, both you and the evaluation staff share an in-depth knowledge of the program area. Therefore, I suggest that you begin by reaching firm agreement on the program areas that should be emphasized and the objectives of the evaluation. Then and only then can you discuss how the evaluation should be conducted.

I believe that your best approach will be to ask the evaluation staff to give you a plan for conducting the evaluation. This plan should contain a number of "operating principles," such as whom they may contact, and under what conditions; dates for interim reports or briefings; types of quantitative and qualitative data wanted; connections to budget and program plans; and method of packaging the findings.

In other words, it is important that you tell the evaluators what is important to you and express your willingness to work with them to help them meet your needs. It may also be helpful to ask the evaluators to give you copies of their previous work plans, intermediate reports, briefing notes, and final documents. In fact, anything that they have produced in the past will provide important specific examples for your negotiations with them.

Once you have received and reviewed the proposed plan, you generally have two basic options: You can negotiate a final plan on your own, or you can ask a third party, an outside evaluation expert, to provide different options or another point of view. If you select the second option, you should make it clear that you want to make sure that the evaluation is as effective as possible, and you are willing to work to that end. In other words, you are simply seeking a noninvolved, third-party view. The third party should be a person who views evaluation as a process that produces no winners or losers. You must also make it clear that the third party will only be providing additional options, not making decisions or siding with either program or evaluation staffers.

Sonnichsen (Chapter Two) points out that the design and conduct of a successful evaluation is significantly dependent on the interpersonal skills of the individual evaluator. By the time you negotiate the evaluation plan, your judgment of the evaluation staff's technical and interpersonal skills should have been verified. If you find that interpersonal skills are lacking, the best you can do (assuming their receptivity to feedback) is to express your concern. This concern should emphasize how evaluation and program staffers were able to communicate during negotiations over the evaluation's objectives and work plan. In stating your concern, it is important that you provide specific examples in a nonevaluative way—that is, you must say what impact different events have had on negotiations. Do not say that the evaluation staff is inept or uninterested in becoming more effective.

Most people who are responsible for program evaluation realize that, in this field, the basic essential interpersonal skill is active listening. Evaluators have to be able to clarify what was said and ask nonthreatening questions so that the facts are clear. They must be able to confirm their understanding of what and why something is said, so that the other parties realize that they are understood. Inability or unwillingness to do this well is often the root cause of evaluators' failure to build good relationships with program managers and their staffs.

Solving a staff's interpersonal-skill problems is not simple. If the evaluation staff responds positively to your feedback and acknowledges deficiencies, you can use a number of approaches to overcome interpersonal deficiencies. There are two very common approaches. First, skill training uses short courses, two to three days long, that allow participants to develop specific interpersonal skills, such as active listening, constructive criticism, and managing differences. Any such course must emphasize practice of the skills, with few lectures. There should also be reinforcing sessions. Of even more benefit is having the evaluation and program staffs participate in the training together. Second, a third-party facilitator can help groups work together effectively. Such a person provides feedback on how individuals and groups are behaving and suggests improvements. This person can be used to help the evaluation-plan negotiation process and can be used as needed during the evaluation.

Obviously, neither of these approaches is a simple solution, but level 2 solutions are not simple. You must decide how important it is to spend time and resources on resolving evaluators' deficiencies. It usually comes down to how important you believe it is to increase the odds of having a meaningful evaluation report, one that will not cause problems in the long run.

Suggestions for Level 1. Because, at this level, you see little or no value in the proposed or ongoing evaluation effort, your tendency will be to help the evaluation staff as little as possible. This inclination will only be intensified, the more deficient the evaluation staff is in technical and interpersonal skills and in program knowledge. Wye (Chapter Four) depicts this tendency by describing a program staff's initial effort to avoid involvement in an evaluation effort at HUD. There are many reasons why you might find yourself in a level 1 situation, but, as a program manager, your primary concern should be what is best for your program and your organization. You may decide that the best approach is to stonewall the evaluation. This may be a legitimate action and the one that best serves the public interest. You may also decide that, given the situation, your best bet is to try to obtain some kind of benefit from the evaluation. If you make this decision, you have probably concluded that you will have more control over the evaluation staff and its findings if you can get the staff to work with you. If so, be candid with the evaluation staff. Be as explicit as possible about your expectations for the evaluation and your concerns about the evaluation staff's competence. At the same time, you have to reassure the evaluators that you are willing to help them ease your concerns. Even if the study has been mandated by legislative or other political elements, your initial focus should be on the goals and objectives of the evaluation. In most cases, the areas to be studied will not be well defined, and so you will have the opportunity to direct the evaluation toward more useful areas. Even if the evaluators are locked in to certain goals or study areas, you may still be able to have them look at other, complementary areas, for a more balanced picture of the program. If this effort proves fruitful, you essentially will have moved the situation to a slightly higher level, and you will be able to use variations of the suggestions provided for levels 2 through 4, assuming some flexibility in time and resources.

One of the keys to your decision about how you will interact with the evaluators is a good relationship with them in the long run. This factor, coupled with the potential impact of the evaluation results, will help you decide on the type of relationship you decide you want with the evaluation staff. In fact, you may find it most pragmatic to work with the evaluation staff along the lines already described, whether or not you view the effort as useful. If you can do nothing else, you may be able at least to delay the evaluation by forcing the evaluation staff to meet your requirements. If they are real requirements, sincerely expressed, the evaluation staff cannot easily fault you for expecting a professional product, professionally and collaboratively produced.

Remember one important thing: for years, evaluators have been frustrated by the general lack of impact of their work. Many articles have been written about this situation, and evaluators are constantly striving to make a difference. By offering to cooperate, and by telling them that you have specific needs and potential uses for their work, you will be offering a very valuable prize.

Some Final Notes

This entire chapter rests on the firm belief that program managers have both the responsibility and the authority to challenge evaluators to work with them and produce professional products useful to them and to other decision makers. It is your right to ensure that the evaluation effort is effective, but you must do this in a way that reflects the kind of behavior you expect from the evaluation staff.

The evaluation staff needs your assistance if it is to be effective. If you view the evaluation process as a way of developing peers with mutual goals, you should be able to push the evaluation staff without being faulted. As long as you behave convincingly while you are trying to create an effective evaluation process, you should get support from people within and outside your program area. Of course, if your organization's climate is such that collaboration among staffs and program units runs counter to normal working relationships, your attempts to encourage collaboration will probably be futile.

You have probably noticed that the lower the level of evaluation readiness, the more you have to use a directive approach toward the evaluation staff. At levels 1 and 2 especially, you have to say very clearly what you expect from the evaluation staff. You have to do this because there is probably some basic insecurity on the part of the staff. In other words, if level 1 or level 2 readiness is appropriate, the evaluation staff is probably both unable and unwilling to take much responsibility for the evaluation effort, because the staff is either incompetent or unconfident. This means that there is probably a power vacuum, and you can and must take a strong leadership role to fill it. Nevertheless, you should keep in mind that your goal is to move the process to the point where a more collaborative approach can be used. As Sonnichsen points out in Chapter Two it falls to evaluators to market both themselves and their product.

Evaluators have to accommodate program managers' views and expectations. They need to realize that, regardless of who initiates an evaluation, program managers will always have the most say over how, when, and if the findings are used. In case a few evaluators have been able to tolerate reading this chapter, I offer the following advice. If you believe that a more collaborative approach to program evaluation leads to more effective results, you have probably seen some of the possibilities for evaluating an evaluation staff. For example, an evaluation staff can be asked to assess itself against task lists in this chapter, indicate what tasks program managers would consider important, and find out from the program managers what tasks they actually believe are most important. Results of these assessments will allow more confident planning.

These are just a few options. Each one provides the opportunity for all parties to understand the others' viewpoints and expectations, allowing those involved to find common ground and begin to develop a collaborative approach to evaluation.

Joseph N. Coffee is chief of the Training Division at the Bureau of Alcohol, Tobacco, and Firearms, U.S. Department of the Treasury. He has held management positions at the Federal Executive Institute, U.S. Information Agency, and the Treasury's Office of the Secretary and Office of Personnel Management. He received his B.A. and M.A. degrees from the University of Virginia.

This chapter presents a framework for examining the process dimensions of evaluation, arraying functional steps against several perspectives.

Process Dimensions in Program Evaluation

Ray C. Oman

The past decade has been traumatic for many American organizations. In the public sector, the early 1980s brought major cutbacks in numerous federal domestic programs. Many of these cutbacks were also extended to state and local governments, which receive funding through their federal counterpart. In contrast, the defense agencies absorbed and managed large budget increases during much of the decade, until recently, when they also began experiencing significant cutbacks. These new directions in funding were the result of changes in priorities and in views of the proper role of government on the part of elected officials and the public at large. All in all, the 1980s have been turbulent times for federal agencies because of wide funding fluctuations and changes in definitions of the proper role of government.

In the private sector, too, the 1980s have been times of major change and new trends. The growing disparity between imports and exports reached new highs, producing a record-breaking balance-of-payments deficit. Many domestic firms saw their traditional markets shrink as competition from foreign firms forced them to reassess their internal management, as well as their strategic relations. A feeling emerged that the United States may have lost its "competitive edge," and there has been a frantic search for ways to regain momentum.

Conditions in the external environment—rapid change, increased competition, and funding shortfalls—have helped to bring such concepts as excellence, quality, and productivity into vogue in most public and private organizations. Program evaluation, along with other social and management sciences, will have an opportunity to contribute to organizations in their search for improvements and new ways to survive and grow. Although growth in program evaluation equal to what occurred in the 1970s seems unlikely, evaluators can probably expect to be called on more and more frequently as organizations are forced to strive for more effectiveness and efficiency. If program evaluation is to reach its full potential as a tool to improve organizations, then the evaluation process, which is concerned with evaluation as an intervention in a social or cultural system, must be given more emphasis.

This chapter presents an exploratory discussion of the evaluation process, in an effort to develop and refine this aspect of program evaluation and to establish common ground for future discussion and refinement. In addition, a rudimentary framework for analyzing the evaluation process is described and then discussed in relation to two models of organizations.

Background

Most reviews of the evaluation literature reveal a more complete treatment of technical methodological issues than of the "softer" process issues, partly because program evaluation is rooted in logical positivism. One of the corollaries of that paradigm is that program evaluation, like the other social sciences, should follow the research approaches of the physical sciences as much as possible. Consequently, the methodological rigor of research has been of more concern than the social, political, and interpersonal interactions that comprise what can be termed the evaluation process. In fact, the process aspect of evaluation is still being defined.

Moreover, the increasing concern with making program evaluation more useful to decision makers has produced a growing interest in how evaluations are conducted and how they can be most useful to decision makers. Thus, over the past ten years, program evaluation has undergone a paradigm shift from primary reliance on logical positivism to an increased appreciation and awareness of the social construction of reality. This shift has brought about the concern for evaluation process and has affected the approaches, tools, and techniques used in evaluations.

There is now increased emphasis on the evaluation process, including the social, cultural, and interpersonal aspects of evaluation, partly because evaluators want to increase evaluation's acceptance and use. Consequently, evaluation process issues, although not fully defined, are of considerable significance to the field, signaling the need for deeper treatment of process considerations.

Many articles and books about the use of evaluation stress such broad concepts as users' involvement and participation, rather than the workings of the evaluation process itself. For example, Waller and others (1979) conclude that users' involvement is in the forefront of other factors affecting utilization: "The only characteristic of an evaluation system associated with utility [is] the degree of involvement of the user in an evaluation activity" (p. 11).

Van de Vall and his collaborators provide somewhat more detail on the evaluation process in their studies of factors affecting the acceptance and implementation of research in industrial organizations in the Netherlands. Their research attempts to use quantitative analysis to identify behavioral variables that are related to acceptance and implementation issues. According to Van de Vall and Bolas (1979), "The impact of social policy research upon organizational decisions is higher when the research sponsor and research consumer are identical or closely linked, rather than consisting of two separate and independent organizations, and . . . [p]rojects of social policy research accompanied by a steering committee consisting of representatives from the research team, the research sponsor, and researcher consumer(s) tend to score higher on policy impact than projects lacking a steering committee." The existence and functioning of a steering committee is an integral part of the study process. A study by Van de Vall, Bolas, and Kang (1976)—of applied research projects in industrial and labor relations, urban planning, and social welfare and health—concludes that the more closely such research projects are adjusted to an organization's current policymaking process, the more easily the results will be utilized.

Oman and Chitwood (1984) extend the inquiry by exploring both structural and behavioral factors that appear to affect the level of acceptance. For the sample of studies that they examined in detail, the authors define behavioral factors as those parts of the study process over which the evaluator has some control, such as choices about methodology, who is involved and in what ways, and how decisions are made on the conduct of the study. In general, their data suggest above-average acceptance of studies in which the analyst and the decision makers (or other personnel in a unit) participate in such key aspects as problem definition, data collection and analysis, and development of conclusions and recommendations.

A Framework for Examining the Evaluation Process

Evaluation methodology is concerned both with substantive and with process components. The substantive component involves such technical aspects as the research design, data-collection methods, analysis, and development of conclusions. For example, the substantive aspects of an evaluation might involve a quasi-experimental design using random sampling and linear multiple regression, with appropriate tests of statistical significance. By comparison, the process component concerns who is involved in making decisions about planning and conducting the evaluation and who carries out the various tasks and activities that comprise the evaluation. Process also involves decisions about how to plan and conduct the evaluation. For example, the process component might involve a chief evaluator who works closely with the decision making in planning but not in conducting the evaluation. No particular substantive component of an evaluation is necessarily right or wrong, and no particular process component is necessarily correct or incorrect. Such judgments must be made on a case-by-case basis, after due consideration of the purpose of an evaluation, among various other factors.

In any case, two key elements of the evaluation process are who is involved and the nature of the interpersonal interaction that characterizes that involvement. For example, an evaluator may have worked closely with a decision maker in defining the purpose of an evaluation, or he or she may have had little contact with the decision maker. If the evaluator did so interact with the decision maker, what was the nature of their work together? For example, did the evaluation begin without a meeting between the decision maker and the evaluator to discuss the purpose of the effort? Did they meet several times and jointly develop a written statement of the purpose of the evaluation?

Obviously, many possible interactions can characterize the process component of any evaluation. Moreover, some aspects of the evaluation process seem quantifiable, while others may not be. Whether there has been a meeting between key actors in an evaluation is a question that can be answered yes or no, but the quality of the meeting may be difficult or impossible to assess. Therefore, only some process dimensions can be categorized or observed. In assessing something as complex as interpersonal processes and interactions, the evaluator must be content with the thought that some knowledge of process is better than none, even if important dimensions remain hidden.

Interpersonal events and interactions that can be used to describe the evaluation process can be divided into two basic categories: those that occur solely among the evaluators, and those that occur between evaluators and clients, decision makers, and other personnel affected by the evaluation. The primary focus of this chapter is the second category.

The framework proposed here for examining the evaluation process is based on the four fundamental steps of the scientific method that characterize most program evaluations: problem definition, data collection, data analysis, and development of conclusions and recommendations. Each of these steps can be examined on two dimensions: (1) who was involved (who participated) and (2) the nature of the event or interaction (the decision was made about conducting the evaluation).

Table 1 shows how such a framework for systematically describing process dimensions can be turned into a worksheet for examining the process of a particular evaluation. These items describe and, to some extent, measure selected interpersonal events and interactions that make up the evaluation process. Essentially, the items are surrogate measures designed to describe who participated in the four key steps of the evaluation and how decisions were made about conducting each step. For example, three parties in most evaluations are the person who requests the evaluation, the personnel in the organizational unit that will be affected by the evaluation, and the evaluator. Decisions about the purpose and the conduct of the evaluation are typically made either by whoever requests the evaluation or by that party in consultation with the evaluator. Thus, the dimensions identified in Table 1 are designed to measure selected aspects of the evaluation process. They include such questions as "Was the problem that the evaluation was supposed to address defined by the decision maker, the evaluator, both, or an interunit study team? Did the evaluator, an interunit study team, or personnel from the evaluated unit analyze and interpret the data?" Answers to such questions indicate the level of involvement and participation of the various parties and allow an evaluation to be placed on a continuum extending from "solitary" to "participative." (For example, evaluations in which the evaluator makes all the decisions about how it will be carried out would be placed on the "solitary" side of the scale.)

Most evaluators agree that there is a positive relationship between the participation of decision makers in a program evaluation and the degree to which its findings are used. Therefore, the evaluation process is particularly important because it governs (and is part and parcel with) participation. The process approach sets the agenda of the evaluation with respect to the level and nature of the interpersonal interactions involved in planning and carrying it out. If the agenda is set on a participatory basis, there will probably be more communication and exchange between evaluators and decision makers than if it is set on a solitary basis.

There is also a relationship between the process and substantive dimensions of evaluation methodology. An evaluation conducted on a more solitary basis, with evaluators having the most say over how it will be carried out, usually emphasizes scientific method and quantitative analyses. Conversely, when decision makers have considerable say over the planning and conduct of an evaluation, it tends to emphasize political process and to be more qualitative.

Evaluation Process and Organizational Models

Besides being aligned with an organization's current process of policymaking (Van de Vall, Bolas, and Kang, 1976), evaluation should take

Table 1. Worksheet for Examining Evaluation Process Dimensions

Process/Participants	Definition of Scope		Data Collection		Data Analysis		Development of Recommendations	
	Plan How	Participate	Plan How	Conduct	Plan How	Conduct	Plan How	Participate
Person(s) requesting the evaluation								
Head evaluator								
Individual evaluator								
Team of evaluators								
Members of interunit study team								
Meetings between evaluator(s) and person(s) requesting the evaluation								
Meetings between evaluator(s) and chief of unit being evaluated								
Meetings between evaluator(s) and personnel from unit being evaluated								

account of the locus of power in the organization. Two basic models of bureaucratic behavior provide a framework for understanding power relationships. First, Weber's (1964) concept of bureaucracies includes an analogy of bureaucracies to hydraulic systems, in which pressure applied at one point in the system is transferred in equal and appropriate amounts to other parts. This concept also posits that bureaucrats follow rules and regulations. More recently, theorists like Berkley (1971) and Silverman (1971) have presented a very different view of organizations. Briefly, these theorists propose that the actions, wants, and needs of individual organizational actors determine the climate and direction taken by the organization.

These models have many implications for determining the approach to an evaluation process. For example, in a bureaucratic organization (as described by Weber), system-optimization approaches would seem most appropriate. Therefore, the evaluator would try to determine how to optimize the overall functioning of the organization. If a change were shown to be best for the organization, the evaluator would not need to be too concerned about its impact on a particular subunit. Alternatively, action theory (as proposed by Silverman) suggests that organizational actors behave in terms of socially defined reality. Further, decisions and actions are the results of the personalities of individual actors and their interaction on any particular issue. In an organization where the whims, likes, dislikes, and power of individual actors determine decisions, the evaluation process may need to optimize organizational subunits' or individual actors' functioning. In either case, the interests of individual actors need to be given prime consideration in this approach.

There are other implications of these theories for the evaluation process. The classic bureaucratic model suggests a concentration of power at the peak of the organizational hierarchy. In organizations that conform to this pattern, the evaluator is less concerned about the involvement and support of organizational actors at lower levels. If the top decision maker can be convinced of the merits of a study recommendation, lower-level organizational actors will follow. If an evaluation is being conducted in an organization that conforms to Silverman's action-theory model, however, decision-making power may be dispersed over several levels. When an organization conforms to this model, it is essential that the evaluator gain the support of decision makers at various levels. It may be necessary to make the evaluation process participative and to involve all the individuals concerned.

Conclusion

Regardless of organizational type and behavior, process should be an important concern in all phases of an evaluation, including its planning, design, conduct, communication, and eventual use of findings. When more than one evaluator is involved (as is normally the case), the evaluation process will reflect interpersonal interactions among the evaluators as well as between evaluators and decision makers. An evaluation team can be run in a participative or a solitary style, and power can be shared or concentrated. The leadership style with which the chief evaluator is most comfortable is a prime consideration.

The evaluator should organize the evaluation process in such a way that its purpose is likely to be achieved. Much thought should go into planning. Who should be involved in the effort, and in what ways? Who should participate in each of the specific phases of the effort, and in what ways? What meetings should be held, when should they be held, and who should be invited? Who should participate in such important decisions as defining the purpose of the evaluation, deciding on its process and substantive methodology, and reviewing recommendations for its acceptance and use? The evaluator does not alone have all the answers to these questions. To be effective, however, the evaluator must have a process agenda. By giving careful attention to process, the evaluator can help ensure that evaluation information gets into the hands of the right decision makers and helps them make their organizations as effective and efficient as their mandates and their environments demand.

References

Berkley, G. E. *The Administration Revolution.* Englewood Cliffs, N.J.: Prentice-Hall, 1971.

Oman, R. C., and Chitwood, S. R. "Management Evaluation Studies: Factors Affecting Acceptance of Recommendations." *Evaluation Review,* 1984, *8* (3), 283–304.

Silverman, D. *The Theory of Organizations.* New York: Basic Books, 1971.

Van de Vall, M. D., and Bolas, C. "The Utilization of Social Policy Research: An Empirical Analysis of Its Structure and Functions." Paper presented at the 74th annual meeting of the Sociological Society, Boston, Aug. 27–31, 1979.

Van de Vall, M. D., Bolas, C., and Kang, T. S. "Applied Social Research in Industrial Organizations: An Evaluation of Functions, Theory, and Methods." *The Journal of Applied Behavioral Science,* 1976, *12* (2), 63.

Waller, J. D., and others. *Developing Useful Evaluation Capability: Lessons from the Model Evaluation Program.* Washington, D.C.: U.S. Department of Justice, 1979.

Weber, M. *The Theory of Social and Economic Organization.* New York: Free Press, 1964.

Ray C. Oman is senior program analyst at the U.S. Army Corps of Engineers headquarters and is responsible for analysis and evaluation studies and information systems planning and assessment. Dr. Oman holds graduate degrees focusing on management science, program evaluation, and public finance from George Washington University and Penn State University.

Index

A

Academics, 39
Accountability, 19
American Evaluation Association (AEA), 3
Analysts, 39
Appropriations process, and evaluation, 30
American Society for Public Administration (ASPA), 2, 3

B

Barkdoll, G. L., 4, 5
Bell, J. B., 4, 5
Berkley, G. E., 77, 78
Bolas, C., 73, 75, 78
Briefings, frequent, 52-53
Bucher, D. E., 13
Budget process, and evaluation, 30

C

Campbell, D., 13
Career government executives, 12-13. *See also* Program managers
Carlson, R. H., 3, 7, 14
Carroll, L., 12
Chelimsky, E., 16, 21, 24-25
Chitwood, S. R., 73, 78
Chlosta, N., 13
Client(s), 1-2; and evaluators, 37; meetings with, 2-3; in team approach, 35-48. *See also* Congressional staff; Political appointee(s); Program managers
Coffee, J. N., 4, 57, 69
Cohen, D. K., 32, 33
Colvard, J. E., 13
Comtois, J., 32, 33
Congress: environment in, 28-29; and evaluation, 27, 29-31; and evaluators, 31-33; and HUD evaluation, 36; micromanagement by, 8-9
Congressional Budget Office (CBO), 9, 28-29
Congressional committees, 28; for HUD programs, 36; influence of, 9
Congressional Research Service (CRS), 28-29
Congressional staff, 1, 3, 28; interviews with, 27, 29-33
Cook, D., 13
Country program review (CPR), 54-55
Crooks, G., 13

D

Data, collection of, 20. *See also* Information
Davis, R., 13

E

Evaluation(s): advice for evaluated in, 57-69; barriers affecting, 8-11; and Congress, 27, 29-31; Congressionally mandated, 31, 32; evaluators' view of, 16; improving, 11-12; and new client, 8; offices for, 19; and political environment, 7; program managers' perspective of, 18-23; team approach to, 35-48; techniques for international, 49-56
Evaluation process, 71-73, 77-78; framework for, 73-75; and organizational models, 75, 77; worksheet for, 76
Evaluation readiness, 62; suggestions for levels of, 63-68
Evaluation staff, 38, 41, 43, 44-48, 58-59
Evaluators: and clients, 37; and Congress, 31-33; constraints from, 29; early, 1; evaluation of, 59-62; evaluation viewed by, 16; forum of, 2-3; and political appointees, 11-12; political principles for, 12; and program managers, 17, 21, 23-24, 68-69; and stress and conflict, 17-18; in team approach, 35-48; techniques for international, 49-56

F

Family Support Act of 1988, 30
Federal Bureau of Investigation, 15
Ferro, F., 13
Fishman, M. E., 3, 27, 33
Forestry project, 53

G

General Accounting Office (GAO), 9, 28-29
General Services Administration, 9
Gormley, W., 51, 56

H

Haag, R., 3, 49, 54, 56
Housing, evaluation of programs for, 36-48

I

India, 50
Information: and Congress, 31; lack of, 9-10; and political appointees, 8, 12; using, 63-67. *See also* Data
International development programs, techniques for evaluating, 3-4, 49-56

K

Kang, T. S., 73, 75, 78
Kelso, J., 12
Kettering, M., 51, 56

L

Legislation: new, 30, 31; reauthorization of, 30, 31-32
Lindbloom, C. E., 32, 33
Livestock control program, 50

M

MITRE Corporation, 15

N

National Institute of Law Enforcement and Criminal Justice, 15
Netherlands, 73
Newcomer, K. E., 2, 4

O

Office of Insured Multifamily Housing Development (OIMHD), 36
Office of Management and Budget, 10
Office of Program Analysis and Evaluation (OPAE), in team approach, 35-48
Office of Technology Assessment (OTA), 9, 29
Oman, R. C., 4, 71, 73, 78
Organizational models, and evaluation process, 75-77
Oversight hearings, 30-31, 32

P

Peace Corps, 54-55
Policy Development and Research (PDR), 35, 47
Political appointee(s), 1, 3; advice from, 11-12; barriers for management by, 8-10; and changing environment, 7; evaluation-related barriers for, 10-11; in forum, 13; information needed by, 8; and interorganizational relationships, 58
Politics, and evaluation, 7-13
Process, in evaluation, 71-78
Program managers, 1, 3; advice to, 58-59; conclusions from, 23-24; evaluation of evaluators by, 59-62; evaluation viewed by, 18-20; and evaluators, 68-69; evaluators' view of, 17; message to evaluators from, 23-24; techniques for international, 49-56; use of information by, 63-67
Program reviews, 54-55
Program staff, 38, 40-48, 58

R

Radin, B. A., 32, 33
Reauthorization, of legislation, 30, 31-32
Researchers, 39
Rosenweig, F., 51, 56

S

Sanera, M., 23, 25
Silverman, D., 77, 78

Sonnichsen, R. C., 3, 15, 16, 22, 25, 66, 68
Southern California, University of (USC), 2, 15
Staff: congressional, 1; evaluation, 38, 41, 43, 44-48, 58-59; program, 38, 40-48, 58; versus line functions, 18-19
Suzuki, M., 13

T

Team approach, to evaluation, 35-48
Team planning meetings (TPMs), 50-52
Triplett, A., 13

U

U.S. Department of Agriculture, 51
U.S. Department of Housing and Urban Development (HUD), in team approach, 35-48

V

Van de Vall, M. D., 73, 75, 78

W

Waller, J. D., 73, 78
Washington Public Affairs Center (WPAC), 2, 8, 15, 22
Water and Sanitation for Health Project, 51
Weber, M., 77, 78
Weiss, C. H., 29, 33
Welfare, 30
Werge, R., 3, 49, 56
Wholey, J. S., 2, 4
Wye, C. G., 3, 35, 48, 67

Y

Young, C. Y., 32, 33

Z

Zweig, F. M., 28, 31, 32, 33